Agricultural Prices, Policy, and Equity in Sub-Saharan Africa

• FOOD IN AFRICA SERIES •

Series Editor: *Art Hansen*
  Center for African Studies
  University of Florida

- Africa's Agrarian Crisis: The Roots of Famine •
  Stephen K. Commins, Michael F. Lofchie, and Rhys Payne, editors

- Food in Sub-Saharan Africa •
  Art Hansen and Della E. McMillan, editors

- Agricultural Prices, Policy, and Equity in Sub-Saharan Africa •
  Dharam Ghai and Lawrence D. Smith

Agricultural Prices, Policy, and Equity in Sub-Saharan Africa

**Dharam Ghai and
Lawrence D. Smith**

*A study prepared for the International Labour Office
within the framework of the World Employment Programme*

Lynne Rienner Publishers, Inc • Boulder, Colorado

The designations employed in ILO publications, which are in conformity with United Nations practice, and the presentation of material therein do not imply the expression of any opinion whatsoever on the part of the International Labour Office concerning the legal status of any country, area or territory or of its authorities, or concerning the delimitation of its frontiers.

The responsibility for opinions expressed in studies and other contributions rests solely with their authors, and publication does not constitute an endorsement by the International Labour Office of the opinions expressed in them.

Reference to names of firms and commercial products and processes does not imply their endorsement by the International Labour Office, and any failure to mention a particular firm, commercial product or process is not a sign of disapproval.

Published in the United States of America in 1987 by
Lynne Rienner Publishers, Inc.
948 North Street, Boulder, Colorado 80302

Library of Congress Cataloging-in-Publication Data

Ghai, Dharam P.
  Agricultural prices, policy, and equity in
Sub-Saharan Africa.

  Bibliography: p.
  Includes index.
  1. Agricultural prices—Africa, Sub-Saharan.
2. Food prices—Africa, Sub-Saharan.   3. Agriculture
and state—Africa, Sub-Saharan.   4. Food supply—
Africa, Sub-Saharan.   I. Smith, Lawrence D.
II. Title.
HD2117.G47 1987   338.1'3'0967   86-20368
ISBN 1-55587-005-8 (lib. bdg.)

Distributed outside of North and South America and Japan by
Frances Pinter (Publishers) Ltd, 25 Floral Street,
London WC2E 9DS England

Printed and bound in the United States of America

The paper used in this publication adheres to the new
American National Standard for Permanence of Paper
for Printed Library Materials, Z39.48-1984.

Contents

Illustrations

• DIAGRAM •

Preface

This book is part of the ongoing research undertaken within the framework of the World Employment Programme of the International Labour Office (ILO). The rural component of the ILO research includes studies on poverty, alternative agrarian systems, access to food, women workers, organizations of the rural poor, participation, migration, and labor markets. A good deal of the recent research has focused on sub-Saharan Africa. Work has been undertaken or is under way on the equity consequences of trends in food prices, on the crisis in agricultural production and access to food, and on the effect of structural adjustment programs on the distribution of employment and income. These investigations have been carried out through in-depth country studies.

The book analyzes the agricultural crisis in Africa with a view to drawing policy conclusions. Thus, Part 1 deals with the nature, dimensions, and causes of agricultural problems. The second part explores in some depth the trends, determinants, and equity consequences of real agricultural prices in the 1970s and early 1980s in sub-Saharan Africa. This part may be considered the main contribution of the book to the ongoing debate on the economic crisis in Africa.

In the course of writing this book many institutions and individuals have been helpful. Some of the material in the book relating to agricultural price trends and their equity consequences was first presented at a conference on Accelerating Food Production in Africa organized in 1983 at Victoria Falls, Zimbabwe, by the International Food Policy Research Institute and the University of Zimbabwe. We are grateful to the participants at the conference and particularly to John Mellor, Michael Lipton, Carl Eicher, Dunstan Spencer, and Christopher Delgado for detailed and stimulating comments that encouraged us to go deeper into price issues, as well as to expand the scope of the work.

One of the authors has worked for a number of years as a consultant for the Food and Agriculture Organization, and the book incorporates a considerable amount of empirical material and a great number of insights obtained as a result of this work. The International Labour Office provided material support and a congenial working atmosphere for carrying out this study. We are grateful to a number of ILO colleagues for support, discussions, and comments. We are indebted to V. Jamal, H. Tabatabai, J. Gaude, J.

Majeres, and G. Farooq for providing detailed comment on an earlier draft. We would also like to thank J. Martin, S. Radwan, A. Ghose, A. Bequele, P. Peek, F. Lisk, R. van der Hoeven, and W. Keddeman for support and helpful comments.

We gratefully acknowledge research assistance from P. Balakrishnan and Vina Jha. Mrs. E. Schaad helped track down documents and publications. For typing successive drafts of the manuscript, we thank Sandra Deacon. Finally, a word of thanks to the Swedish Agency for Research Cooperation with Developing Countries (SAREC) for funding part of the research costs.

Dharam Ghai
Lawrence D. Smith

The World Employment Programme (WEP) was launched by the International Labour Organisation in 1969, as the ILO's main contribution to the International Development Strategy for the Second United Nations Development Decade.

The means of action adopted by the WEP have included the following:

- short-term high-level advisory missions;
- longer-term national or regional employment teams; and
- a wide-ranging research programme.

Through these activities the ILO has been able to help national decision-makers to reshape their policies and plans with the aim of eradicating mass poverty and unemployment.

A landmark in the development of the WEP was the World Employment Conference of 1976, which proclaimed inter alia that "strategies and national development plans should include as a priority objective the promotion of employment and the satisfaction of the basic needs of each country's population." The Declaration of Principles and Programme of Action adopted by the Conference will remain the cornerstone of WEP technical assistance and research activities during the 1980s.

This publication is the outcome of a WEP project.

·1·

Introduction

Widespread starvation, hunger, and malnutrition in Ethiopia, Sudan, and a number of other African countries have suddenly riveted world attention on the agricultural and food situation in sub-Saharan Africa. The tragedy of deaths and suffering from famines has provoked a wide-ranging debate on the nature, origin, and causes of this crisis. It is clear that if Africa is to be spared the nightmare of recurring hunger and prolonged malnutrition, policy and action must be based on a correct identification of the nature and underlying causes of the present problems. The recent upsurge in investigation and analysis of the crisis has made some contribution; yet the situation is so complex, the data base so weak, and our knowledge so limited that there is a pervasive dissatisfaction with the profundity and rigor of much of the analytical work done so far and a persistent feeling that a lot more work needs to be done in data gathering and analysis, particularly at the local and national levels, in order to achieve a satisfactory understanding of the many factors that have contributed to the present situation.

The present monograph represents an effort toward better understanding of African agricultural problems. It has two main objectives: first, to treat somewhat more systematically the issues of the nature, dimensions, and causes of agricultural problems (discussed in Part 1), and secondly, to explore in some depth one aspect of this phenomenon—namely, the trends, determinants, and equity consequences of real agricultural prices in the 1970s and early 1980s in sub-Saharan Africa (discussed in Part 2). Our emphasis on agricultural prices should not be interpreted to mean that we subscribe to the view that the prices are the only or even the most important determinant of agricultural performance. Our discussion of agricultural prices has the more limited purpose of documenting the trends in real prices of food and export crops and exploring the relatively neglected theme of the equity impact of such price trends.

To introduce the subsequent discussion the next chapter deals with the nature and dimensions of the crisis. While there has been a great deal of talk

1

recently about "the African crisis," there is much less clarity and agreement on its manifestations and dimensions. Various commentators have interpreted the "crisis" in different and often contradictory terms. The next chapter treats in a more systematic manner the various manifestations of the crisis, to identify its core elements and to quantify their dimensions and direction of change. The crisis is manifested variously in hunger and poverty, slowdown of overall economic growth, poor agricultural performance, widening gap between food demand and domestic availability, stagnation or slow growth in agricultural exports, high rates of rural-urban migration, rapidly increasing agricultural imports, and rising food prices. Perhaps the central element in the crisis is low and insufficient growth in labor productivity; its manifestations enumerated above may relate back to this aspect.

In popular discussions of the subject, not only are the manifestations and dimensions of the crisis portrayed in simplistic terms but the entire region is treated as one unit with similar problems and performance. This is a gross oversimplification of reality and is likely to result in misleading policy prescriptions and action programs. While there are indeed many common elements in the region, what is perhaps more remarkable is the diversity of situations and experiences. This demonstration of diversity is the main purpose of Chapter 3, which deals successively with differences among African countries with respect to structure and growth of the economy, food and export crop production, labor productivity, and agricultural imports. The chapter also examines striking diversity in such resource parameters as climate and soils, food systems, arable land, and labor force.

Not only is this diversity overlooked in discussions of the African crisis but there is also a tendency to ascribe the crisis to simple, often superficial causes. We may mention the singling out of low and declining food and export crop prices as "the" (or the most important) cause of poor agricultural performance in Africa. Others have highlighted the role of population growth, environmental deterioration, weather, political disturbances, limited technological progress, etc. Chapter 4 aims to examine the various hypotheses that have been put forward to explain the African agricultural crisis and to assess their validity in the light of the available evidence.

Part 2 focuses on the trends in and equity consequences of real agricultural prices. The justification for selecting prices for in-depth discussion is threefold. First, issues of price trends and policies have been stressed repeatedly by a large number of analysts as a key to understanding the African crisis. Secondly, more reliable data are available on prices for a relatively long period of time than for many other variables. Thirdly, while there has been a good deal of discussion on the relationship between agricultural prices and production, there has been very little systematic analysis of their equity implications.

In spite of the heavy emphasis laid on prices as a key tool of agricultural policy, there appears to be little appreciation of the limitations constraining the realization of its full potential in the concrete setting of African economies. Chapter 5 makes an assessment of the possibilities and limitations of prices as an instrument of economic policy, taking into account such features of the African economies as the significant weight of subsistence activities, institutional bottlenecks to functioning of product and factor markets, weak transport and infrastructural facilities, lack of skilled manpower and information, dispersion of responsibility for policy making, inadequate coverage of marketing activities, etc.

The next chapter assembles data on consumer and producer prices for a range of agricultural commodities for a large number of African countries during the period 1968–1980. It estimates trends in consumer food prices, producer food prices, and export crops and compares them with the world prices for these products. The chapter thus provides one set of price trend estimates that can be compared with others, or rather with general statements about price trends based on somewhat sketchy evidence and incomplete data. The material in the chapter can perhaps supply the empirical foundations for in-depth analysis of the economic impact of movements in agricultural prices.

The two succeeding chapters move the discussion from the regional to the country level and inject the equity dimensions. Chapter 7 gives flesh and blood to the continental skeleton by examining in some detail six country experiences with respect to agricultural price trends, marketing structures and policies, and the main determinants of the trends in agricultural prices. This provides an opportunity to look at the central thrusts of government policy on agricultural prices as well as to assess the relative importance of different mechanisms in influencing prices, such as exchange rates, export taxes, marketing board surpluses and subsidies, and efficiency of the marketing system. The discussion highlights similarities and diversities in marketing structures and policies and in mechanisms used to influence agricultural prices.

Chapter 8 focuses on the equity implications of agricultural price trends. After a brief description of the main features of the equity situation in African countries, the chapter develops and applies a framework to assess the equity impact in several African countries of trends in consumer food prices. A tentative analysis of the main equity implications of the trends in producer prices follows. The concluding section gives a more detailed analysis of the equity impact of agricultural prices through a discussion of four country experiences. The concluding chapter highlights the principal findings of the study, assesses their implications for policy and action, and suggests some priority areas for investigation and analysis.

·PART 1·
Dimensions and Causes of Crisis

· 2 ·

The Nature and Dimensions of the Agricultural Crisis

The agricultural crisis in sub-Saharan Africa is not a simple problem nor does it stem from a single cause. On the contrary, its many facets and the variety of factors that may have contributed to the present situation make its analysis extremely complicated. The paucity and unreliability of much of the available data hinder study of the problem, as does the fact that the region, as defined by the World Bank and as used in this volume, consists of 39 countries, excluding the smaller off-shore islands.

In this chapter we examine, at the regional or aggregate level, the published evidence on various facets of the crisis such as the level of hunger and poverty, various indicators of agricultural production, and the level of agricultural incomes. The consequences of rural-urban migration and output instability are considered, and the combined effect of these various factors on agricultural imports and food prices is then examined.

· THE ECONOMIC GROWTH OF THE REGION ·

Almost immediately one is confronted with gaps in the official statistics. Some countries do not have published national income figures for all years, and there are several conceptual problems in converting data from different countries into a single growth rate for a group of countries. Nevertheless, the World Bank and the International Monetary Fund (IMF) have both attempted to construct time series of the real growth rates of gross domestic product (GDP).

The World Bank has produced time series specifically for the sub-Saharan African region, subdividing the countries by level of income and the presence of oil production (Table 2.1). The World Bank definition of this region excludes South Africa. Unfortunately, the data are separated into two time periods only, but the 1970s compared with the 1960s have seen a deterioration in the regional rate of growth of real GDP from 3.8 to 3.0 percent

Table 2.1 Rates of Growth of Real GDP and Real GDP Per Head in Sub-Saharan Africa

	Rate of Growth of GDP		Percent Per Year Rate of Growth of Population		Implicit Rate of Growth of GDP Per Head	
	1960-70	1970-82	1960-70	1970-82	1960-70	1970-82
Low income economies	4.0	1.8	2.4	2.8	1.6	−1.0
Low income semi-arid	2.4	2.6	2.5	2.6	−0.1	0
Low income other	4.2	1.7	2.4	2.9	1.8	−1.2
Middle income oil importers	4.2	3.7	2.7	3.3	1.5	0.4
Middle income oil exporters	3.5	4.1	2.4	2.6	1.1	1.5
Sub-Saharan Africa	3.8	3.0	2.4	2.8	1.4	0.2
All low income countries	4.5	4.5	2.3	1.9	2.2	2.6
All lower middle-income countries	4.9	5.3	2.5	2.5	2.4	2.8

Source: World Bank, *Toward Sustained Development in Sub-Saharan Africa* (Washington, D.C., 1984), Annex Tables 2 and 25.

per year, compared with a constant 4.5 percent per year for the world's low income countries in general and an increase from 4.9 to 5.3 percent per year in income growth for the world's lower middle income countries. Moreover, the high rate of population growth in the region means that there was virtually no growth in GDP per head over the 1970s in sub-Saharan Africa in general. Performance did vary by groups of countries within the region, however, with the middle income countries, particularly the oil-exporters, having a more favorable GDP growth rate in the 1970s than the low income economies.

The World Bank also presents estimates of the average annual real rate of growth for "Africa south of the Sahara" (Table 2.2). This series has the disadvantage of including South Africa, whose economy, together with that of Nigeria, completely dominates the performance of the region. Nevertheless, it has the advantage that the series extends back to the 1950s. Furthermore, the 1960s are disaggregated into five-year time periods. Unfortunately, the 1970s are not disaggregated, and so the effect of the oil price shock cannot be clearly distinguished.

The advantage of examining this series is that it suggests that the growth in GDP and the GDP per head has been slowing down since the mid 1960s, unlike the south Asian region or developing countries in general. Moreover, except in 1960–1965 the rate of growth in the region has generally been lower than in other developing countries. As South Africa has had a higher growth rate than the region in general since the 1960s, its exclusion would have worsened sub-Saharan Africa's performance relative to that of other countries. Agriculture's significant role in the regional economy suggests that the agricultural crisis may have been building up over the past twenty years.

The IMF produces an annual series of the rate of growth of GDP at constant prices for the "non-oil developing countries of Africa," which has the advantage that the influence of particular events can be examined in more detail. The disadvantage is that besides including South Africa it also includes Morocco and Tunisia while excluding Nigeria. However, taking a six-year moving average to smooth out annual fluctuations, from Diagram 2.1 it appears that while this group of countries enjoyed a relatively impressive and slowly improving growth rate of between 5.0 and 5.2 percent per year over the period 1960–1965 to 1966–1971, from then on, and even before the first major oil price rise, the growth rate fell almost continuously so that by 1974–1979 it was as low as 1.8 percent per year. This confirms the long-term nature of the poor economic performance of the region. The commodity boom of the 1975–1977 period gave some respite, with growth rates rising temporarily to 3.1 percent per year in 1976–1981; but since then, with the onset of the world recession, the moving average has fallen to only 2.6 percent per year in 1978–1983, and the negative growth rates of 1982–1983 suggest that the moving average has yet farther to fall. Again, the IMF statistics suggest that the performance of this group of African countries compares unfavorably with that of non-oil developing countries in general.

The general impression, then, is of a region whose GDP growth has been declining for a substantial period and whose high and accelerating population growth rate has led to an even lower GDP growth per head. In 1982 the average GNP per head for the sub-Saharan region was estimated at only $491, with an average per head income of $249 in the twenty-three low income countries of the region, $634 in the eleven middle-income oil importers, and $889 in the five middle-income oil exporters.[1]

Table 2.2 Average Annual Real Growth Rates of GDP and GDP Per Head

	GDP Percentage Per Year			
	1950-60	1960-65	1965-70	1970-81
Africa, South of Sahara	3.5	5.2	4.8	3.3
South Asia	3.9	4.3	4.9	3.8
Developing countries	4.6	5.1	6.0	5.2
South Africa	2.9[a]	6.5	5.8	3.7
	GDP Per Head Percentage Per Year			
	1950-60	1960-65	1965-70	1970-81
Africa, South of Sahara	1.2	2.7	2.3	0.4
South Asia	2.0	1.9	2.5	1.6
Developing economies	2.4	2.6	3.5	2.8
South Africa	0.6[a]	4.1	3.4	0.9

[a]1953–60 only

Source: World Bank, *World Tables*, 3rd ed., Series III (Washington, D.C., 1983), Table 1.

Diagram 2.1 Average Annual Compound Growth Rate of GDP at Constant Prices—Six-Year Moving Average

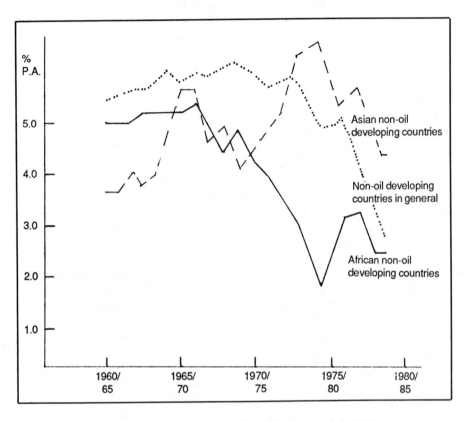

Source: IMF, *International Financial Statistics Yearbook* (Washington, D.C., 1984), pp. 120–121.

• HUNGER AND POVERTY •

It is self-evident that such a low level of per head GNP and such a poor growth would lead to widespread poverty and hunger, especially in the low income countries, and this is confirmed by the limited data available. The Food and Agriculture Organization (FAO) has estimated that some seventy million people or about 18 percent of the population in the sub-region were seriously undernourished in 1981,[2] and the World Bank estimates the number of severely hungry and malnourished people to have increased from close to eighty million in 1972–1974 to as many as 100 million in 1984.[3]

At the regional level, there has been a deficit in the calorie supply per head of between 9 and 12 percent for over two decades (Table 2.3). Perhaps surprisingly there is no indication of any marked deterioration in the situation at the regional level over this period. One explanation is that up to the present increasing food imports have offset declining per head domestic production. Whether this trend can continue in the future is extremely doubtful.

In the early 1960s the calorie supply situation was most serious in the middle-income oil exporters with the deficit in other groups of countries ranging between 4 and 6 percent. In recent years the situation appears to have improved in middle-income countries, but it has deteriorated markedly in the low-income economies. Of course, these are country group averages, which disguise the disparities in calorie availability both within and between countries.

The continuing nature of this shortage of food perhaps needs emphasizing. The human suffering so clearly visible in televised reports of drought-related famines diverts attention away from the chronic state of undernourishment that is continuously present in much of the region. In many countries, and for a significant proportion of the population, hunger is not something that will go away once the rains come.

The most vivid and appalling consequences of famines are the human casualties and the deterioration of health, but the problems extend beyond these. In the wake of famines come also political and social instability; jeopardy to national political independence of those countries heavily dependent on food donations or purchases; the ill effects of prolonged food shortages and deficiencies on morale, motivation, and productivity; the accentuation of social inequalities; and the large-scale human and animal migrations associated with famines that can destabilize the economies of the recipient countries. [4]

Poverty for the individual stems from one of three causes. First, the individual or the family may be unable to produce sufficient goods and services to meet their own needs. This may be due to ignorance, lack of entre-

Table 2.3 Calorie Supply Per Head as a Percentage of Daily Requirements in Sub-Saharan Africa

Classification	1961–65	1970	1975	1981
Low income economies	94	94	89	86
Low income semi-arid	95	88	84	88
Low income other	94	95	90	86
Middle-income oil importers	96	97	96	100
Middle-income oil exporters	84	83	82	91
Sub-Saharan Africa	91	91	88	90

Source: World Bank, *World Tables*, 3rd ed. (Washington, D.C., 1983), Social Data Sheet 1 (Baltimore: The Johns Hopkins University Press, 1984); and World Bank, *Toward Sustained Development*, Table 29.

preneurship, or lack of adequate resources such as land, water, or human effort because of ill-health and the presence of debilitating disease. Secondly, there may be an inability to obtain these minimum needs through exchange either of goods produced by the family or resources owned by the family such as labor. Thirdly, the public or private provision of welfare goods and services to those in need may be inadequate.

In economies whose major source of livelihood is farming and in which agriculture constitutes a significant proportion of GDP, the link between hunger, poverty and agricultural performance is readily seen. In the sub-Saharan African region with an average per head income of $491 in 1982, 72 percent of the labor force is still engaged in agriculture and 78 percent of the population still lives in rural areas,[5] and yet agriculture accounts for only 33 percent of the region's GDP. Among twenty-four African countries for which we have estimates of the extent of rural poverty in the 1970s, in 17 poverty affected more than 50 percent of the population. In only one country (Mauritius) did the level fall below 35 percent.[6]

Given a generally low level of productivity in the agricultural sector, the farmers with least resources and/or lowest productivity will have difficulty supplying their own needs, and the agricultural sector will generate few, if any, rewarding employment opportunities. Nor will the agricultural sector generate much spending power in the rural areas even though domestic food prices are likely to be high unless ample food imports can be afforded or arranged. The high food prices will adversely affect both urban and rural populations relying on purchased foodstuffs. Moreover, the taxable yield of the agricultural sector will be restricted and the potential for welfare provision by the government severely circumscribed.

Even though the role of the agricultural sector tends to decline in relative importance over time as economies grow, the performance of the agricultural sector plays a major role in influencing the extent and degree of poverty and hunger in the region.

• SOME INDICATORS OF AGRICULTURAL PRODUCTION •

The rate of growth of agricultural GDP is unrecorded for many countries, particularly for the 1960s, due to the subsistence nature of much of agricultural production and the undeveloped state of national income accounting in several countries. The FAO, however, produces annual estimates of the aggregate volume of agricultural and food production in each country, and weighted averages for the sub-Saharan region, shown in Table 2.4, have been produced from these estimates. These clearly show the decline in the growth of total agricultural production in the 1970s compared with the 1960s, leading to a negative growth rate of per head agricultural and food

Table 2.4 Weighted Average Annual Growth of Volume of
Production (Percent)

	Total			
	Total Agriculture		Food	
	1960–70	1970–82	1960–70	1970–82
Low-income economies	3.1	0.7	3.2	1.0
Low-income semi-arid	2.3	2.8	2.1	2.8
Low-income other	3.2	0.6	3.3	0.9
Middle-income oil importers	3.8	2.5	3.7	3.3
Middle-income oil exporters	1.1	2.3	1.1	2.4
Sub-Saharan Africa	2.5	1.4	2.5	1.7
	Per Head			
Low-income economies	0.9	−1.4	1.0	−1.2
Low-income semi-arid	−0.2	−0.1	−0.5	−0.1
Low income other	1.1	−1.6	1.2	−1.4
Middle-income oil importers	0.7	−1.2	0.7	−0.6
Middle-income oil exporters	−1.4	−0.7	−1.4	−0.3
Sub-Saharan Africa	0.2	−1.1	0.2	−0.9

Source: World Bank, *Towards Sustained Development*, Table 21.

production in the 1970s. Overall growth was particularly poor in the low-income (other) countries, leading to a substantial rate of decline in per head production. Even the reasonable overall growth rate of food production of 3.3 percent per year in the middle-income oil importers in 1970–1982 resulted in a negative per head growth rate because of the high rate of population growth.

Some people argue that this declining per head food production is the nub of the agricultural crisis facing the region. Over the period 1960–1982, population in this vast subregion of Africa has been growing at 2.6 percent per year, the highest rate in the world, while food production has been growing at only 2.1 percent per year. Sub-Saharan Africa has the dubious distinction of being the only region of the world where per head food production has been declining over this period.[7] Moreover, in the past few years the situation has continued to deteriorate, with the region's food production per head in 1980–1982 falling 5 percent below the 1974–1976 level whereas in all developing countries it rose on average by over 6 percent.[8]

Food production for domestic consumption is not the only component of agricultural production. Traditionally countries in the region have relied on exports of cash crops such as coffee, cocoa, and cotton; food crops such as groundnuts; and in some countries livestock products as a major source of export earnings. However, in volume terms agricultural exports were no higher in 1977–1979 than in 1961–1963, and over the period 1971–1980 the volume of exports fell by 3.5 percent per year.[9] Virtually all agricultural products except tea, sugar, and tobacco (as well as hides and skins) showed a decline in export volume over the 1970s and in most instances real prices also fell over this period (Table 2.5).

Table 2.5 Volumes and Real Prices of Major Agricultural Exports

	Average Annual Change in Volume (Percent)		Annual Average Growth of Real Price (Percent)	
	1961/63 to 1969/71	1969/72 to 1980/82ᵃ	1961–70	1970–82
Cocoa	0.2	–0.3	4.9	3.0
Coffee	3.4	–0.2	0.3	1.8
Tea	9.0	4.1	–4.5	–2.8
Sugar	3.2	1.4	–5.3	–2.7
Groundnut oil	2.2	–6.0	0.1	–4.0
Oilseed cake and meal	5.3	–3.8	0.6	–4.1
Palm oil	–8.6	–5.1	–2.3	–3.2
Bananas	–1.7	–5.4	0.1	–1.1
Maize	–1.9	–5.1	–0.2	–4.2
Cotton	5.6	–3.5	–1.7	–1.9
Tobacco	–3.1	6.6	3.0	–1.2
Rubber	3.0	–2.9	–4.6	0.0
Sisal	–2.1	–8.7	–8.4	0.1

ᵃ End-point growth rates
Source: World Bank, *Toward Sustained Development*, Tables 24 and 12.

In many countries this poor export performance has severely constrained the ability to import commodities required for development without encountering balance of payments difficulties or the need to borrow
funds from overseas. Even though the contribution of the agricultural sector
to GDP fell from 49 percent in 1960 to 33 percent in 1982, agriculture is still
a major component of the economy of the subregion and this poor performance obviously depressed the overall growth rate of the economy.

• AGRICULTURAL INCOMES AND URBANIZATION •

Despite this slow growth in agricultural production and the decline in its
contribution to GDP, agriculture still supplies the livelihood for the majority
of the working population. However, with agriculture's share of GDP falling
faster than its share of working population, the implication is that agricultural incomes have not risen as rapidly as non-agricultural incomes.

With such a large proportion of the population engaged in agriculture,
the degree of urbanization is very low and accounted for only 11 percent of
the population in 1960.[10] But the exodus from the rural areas over the past
two decades has been such that the average annual urban population
growth rate was 5.3 percent in the 1960s and 5.9 percent in the 1970s, so that
by 1980, 21 percent of the population was urbanized.[11] This has had several
implications for agriculture.

The first is that the urbanization is being fueled to a large extent by the migration of young and educated people from the rural areas, depriving the agricultural industry, which is still extremely labor-intensive in its operations, of its potential labor force and increasing the average age of the remaining labor force. The result is that in all countries the size of the effective agricultural labor force, although growing in absolute terms, has grown less rapidly than the total population relying on agriculture for its livelihood. This implies that on average each working member of a farm family has more mouths to feed on the farm than previously. Moreover, as the effective agricultural labor force has grown even less rapidly than the total population, this raises the food dependency ratio even higher.

This leads to the second implication of rapid urbanization, that the demand for *marketed* food has grown very rapidly. A 5.9 percent urban growth rate sustained for twelve years doubles the demand for food in the urban areas, assuming a constant per head income. Even if the food was being produced in sufficient quantities in the rural areas, a large and continuing investment in transport and marketing infrastructure would be required to mobilize supplies for the urban areas. In Chapter 4 it is argued that a contributory cause to the crisis may be the failure to invest sufficiently in transport infrastructure and storage facilities.

At the same time the demand for food in the urban areas has been rising, the increasing absolute size of the rural population has been creating problems particularly in those countries where the population pressure on the available arable land is severe. In much of the region the traditional method of farming has been some variation of the "slash and burn" system, whereby forest or bush is cleared and cultivated for a few years until its fertility declines, and then the area is left for several years to regenerate itself. Increased population pressure eventually reduces the length of the recuperative phase until fertility cannot be sustained. Given the fragility of the soil types of much of Africa, with their low humus content, removal of the tree cover and woody vegetation to increase the arable area or for fuel, together with overcropping and overgrazing, can rapidly lead to desertification. Even in those areas where suitable settled farming systems have been devised, increased population pressure can lead to a marked subdivision and fragmentation of the available land and/or the migration of people in search of land. In many cases the only land available is in areas of low and extremely variable rainfall, and farming in these areas is subject to a high degree of risk.

We thus have the paradoxical situation that with the existing labor-intensive technologies it is difficult to raise labor productivity. Hence an increase in the effective labor force or labor–augmenting capital investment is essential in order to increase output substantially. However, where potentially cultivable land is scarce, a rapidly rising rural population poses a threat of environmental damage and falling labor productivity with the existing technologies. There is thus a pressing need throughout the region to find farming systems and technologies that raise labor productivity, as well as new systems that raise land productivity in the more densely populated areas.

• SHORT-TERM INSTABILITY OF OUTPUT •

Superimposed on the secular decline in the rate of growth of the per head food production and the stagnant export performance are frequent and wide fluctuations in short-term food and cash crop production due to climatic, particularly rainfall, variation. This rainfall variability is not a new phenomenon; indeed, the catastrophic drought in the Sahelian countries in the early 1970s was the twentieth major drought in that area since the 16th century.[12] Usually droughts occur somewhere in Africa every year. Two or more droughts affecting large areas occur about every decade, with extremely protracted and widespread droughts every thirty years. Under traditional systems practiced with low population pressures (relative to the carrying capacity of the land) there was a certain degree of resilience in the farming system reinforced by the social structure. However, increasingly the delicate balance among the physical environment, population, technology, and social structures and systems is breaking down so that droughts are triggering acute food shortages and a reduction in cash incomes to purchase the limited food available.

• AGRICULTURAL IMPORTS •

The widening food production-consumption gap, together with most governments' desires to attempt to feed adequately the rapidly growing urban population, has led to increasing quantities of imports into sub-Saharan Africa. The dramatic and accelerating increase in the volume and value of imports over the past two decades, albeit from a low base in relation to total food consumption, is shown in Table 2.6. Cereals are clearly the largest single component of the agricultural import bill. During the 1960s the volume of cereal imports rose 9 percent per year, but this increased to 12.3 percent per year over the period 1969–1971 to 1980–1982. Over the most recent period (1977–1979 to 1980–1982), the volume of cereal imports rose at a rate of 19.9 percent per year. Imports of all three major cereals—wheat, rice, and maize—rose rapidly, but imports of rice, the largest constituent of cereal imports in the early 1960s, have risen less rapidly than imports of wheat or

Table 2.6 Agricultural Imports by Sub-Saharan African Countries (Volume of Gross Imports)

Commodity	'000 Metric Tons Per Year				Average Annual Growth Rate (Percent)		Value of Imports Millions of Dollars Per Year			
	1961–63	1969–71	1977–79	1980–82	1961–63 to 1969–71	1969–71 to 1980–82	1961–63	1969–71	1977–79	1979–83
Total agricultural imports							749	1,137	4,227	6,573
Total cereals	1,177	2,346	4,862	8,373	9.0	12.3	114	225	1,234	2,225
Wheat	394	1,043	2,352	4,146	12.9	13.4	30	81	473	945
Rice	464	680	1,696	2,317	4.9	11.8	63	91	619	910
Maize	197	385	599	1,635	8.7	14.1	12	32	102	372
Sugar	670	816	1,281	1,596	2.5	6.3	84	109	429	824
Dairy products							44	109	457	643
Animal and vegetable fats and oils	51	122	325	690	11.5	17.1	12	32	204	453

Source: FAO, Trade Yearbook (Rome: FAO, various years).

maize over the past two decades. Sugar imports have not risen as rapidly as cereals, but even so the annual growth rate has increased from 2.5 percent per year in the 1960s to 6.3 percent in the 1970s, and 7.6 percent over the period 1977–1979 to 1980–1982. Although it is difficult to obtain a meaningful volume figure for dairy products, in value terms imports have risen very rapidly over the past two decades, with a rate of growth of 12 percent per year in the 1960s and 17.5 percent in the 1970s. However, in the most recent period (1977–1979 to 1980–1982), the rate slowed slightly but was still extremely high at 12.1 percent per year. The most dramatic rate of increase in major agricultural imports has been in the volume of animal and vegetable fats and oils, with increases of 11.5 percent in the 1960s, 17.1 percent in the 1970s, and 28.5 percent per year over the period of 1977–1979 to 1980–1982. The impression is sometimes given that all food imports into the region are food aid imports obtained on concessional terms, but this is far from true. In the period 1980–1982 food aid imports amounted to just over 2 million tons of grain equivalent which represented just under one quarter of total cereal imports.

There are, of course, many different factors influencing this increase in imports and these will be discussed later. However, there are two features that disturb most commentators. The first is whether these increases are sustainable, given the weak balance of payments situations of many countries and fluctuations in the availability of world supplies. Over the 1970s food imports as a percentage of total export earnings grew at 1.3 percent per year.[13] The need to import food can divert foreign exchange from other imports essential for development—including agricultural inputs and consumer goods, which can act as stimulants and incentives to agricultural production—and hence further slow down the rate of growth of output.

The second feature is the increasing trend in imports and consumer tastes toward commodities like wheat that are technically or economically extremely difficult to grow in much of Africa. At the same time, while these trends in imports are alarming, many sub-Saharan countries are still exporting food commodities, and the level of *net* food imports by the region during the 1970s represented less than 4 percent of total consumption, relatively small compared with the levels of other net food importing regions of the Third World.[14] This point needs stressing because there is a frequent confusion between cereal imports and supplies and food imports and supplies. In 1961–1965 cereals accounted for 54 percent of calorie production in sub-Saharan Africa and less than 53 percent in 1976–1980.[15] Several unduly alarmist reports of the actual food situation in the region have arisen from this confusion.[16]

• RISING FOOD PRICES •

One of the consequences of the food production-consumption gap and the rapid increase in urbanization has been a marked increase in the price of food relative to the cost of living in most countries in the region. Of seventeen countries for which reasonably comprehensive data for the 1970s could be obtained, in thirteen the Food Price Index was growing statistically significantly faster (at the 0.1 level) than the Consumer Price Index (Table 2.7).[17] Food price increases were a major cause of urban inflation over this decade and a contributory factor to the declining standard of living of many urban people, especially the poor and those whose nominal wages were constrained by government legislation.

• SUMMARY •

The poor agricultural performance and the general slowdown in the region's overall growth are obviously closely connected. This combination leads to particular problems of poverty and hunger in both the rural and the urban areas as inadequate food supplies lead to rising food prices. Agricultural trade has also been affected. There has been a squeeze on foreign exchange generation stemming from the reduced volume of agricultural exports, and scarce foreign exchange is being used to purchase food imports. All of these facets of the crisis seem to stem from one basic factor, the continuing low level of agricultural productivity in the region. This chronic situation, which has persisted for probably two decades, has been intensified by the problems created by the recent world recession and by a series of droughts in various parts of the Continent but particularly in the Sahelian

Table 2.7 Annual Percentage Growth in the Food Price Index to the Consumer Price Index Over the Period 1969–1980

Country	Percentage growth rate	Country	Percentage growth rate
Burundi	-0.03^{ns}	Niger	1.02
Cameroon	1.17	Senegal	1.11
Ethiopia	1.26	Sierra Leone	1.21
Ghana	2.51	Swaziland	0.51^{ns}
Côte–d'Ivoire	1.35	United Republic of Tanzania	1.71
Liberia	0.61	Togo	0.78
Madagascar	0.81	Zambia[a]	0.57
Malawi	0.82	Zimbabwe[a]	-0.31
Mauritius	-0.07^{ns}		

[a] 1970–80 only
ns Not statistically significant at the 0.1 level

Source: ILO, *Yearbook of Labour Statistics* (Geneva: ILO, various years).

region. The reasons for this situation and some of the lessons that may be learned from it will be explored in the ensuing chapters.

• NOTES •

1. World Bank, *Towards Sustained Development in Sub-Saharan Africa* (Washington, D.C., 1984), Table 1. The World Bank warns that the GNP per head figures must be interpreted with great caution because of data and conversion factor problems it hopes to be able to remedy in future years.

2. FAO, *State of Food and Agriculture 1981* (Rome: FAO, 1982), p. 75.

3. World Bank, *Towards Sustained Development,* p. 9.

4. OAU, *Famine in Africa* (Rome: FAO, 1982), p. 9.

5. World Bank, *Towards Sustained Development,* Table 27.

6. FAO, *Development Strategies for the Rural Poor* (Rome: FAO, 1984), Table 2, p. 93.

7. While Table 2.4 suggests that the negative growth rate for per head food production is confined to the 1970–1982 period, USDA estimates suggest a negative growth rate for the 1960–1970 period. See USDA, *Food Problems and Projects in Sub-Saharan Africa: The Decade of the 1980s,* ERS, Foreign Agricultural Research Report No. 1966 (Washington, D.C., 1981), pp. 57–60.

8. Calculated from FAO, *Production Yearbook 1982,* Tables 3 and 19.

9. FAO, *State of Food and Agriculture,* Annex Table 8.

10. World Bank, *Accelerated Development in Sub-Saharan Africa: An Agenda for Action* (The Berg Report) (Washington, D.C., 1981), Table 36.

11. Ibid.

12. OAU, *Famine in Africa,* p. 9.

13. FAO, *State of Food and Agriculture,* Table 14.

14. L. Paulino, "The Evolving Food Situation in Sub-Saharan Africa," Paper presented at a Conference on Accelerating Agricultural Production in Sub-Saharan Africa, Victoria Falls, Zimbabwe, September 1983.

15. Ibid.

16. For instance, "Some 130 million of Africa's 515 million people will be sustained by foreign grain this year," in *U.S. News and World Report,* 3 December 1984.

17. See Appendix 1, Chapter 6 of this book.

·3·

The Diversity of Experience

$\mathbf{A}$s we have seen, at the regional level sub-Saharan Africa is facing a series of agricultural crises. But are the problems the same in each country? It is important to appreciate that sub-Saharan Africa is a vast and diverse region consisting, depending on definitions, of up to forty-six countries. For our present purposes the off-shore islands, with the exception of Madagascar, will not be studied, nor will the two smallest mainland countries of Equatorial Guinea and Djibouti. South Africa is also excluded. This leaves the thirty-nine countries listed in Table 3.1 to be examined. These countries vary considerably in terms of historical background, culture, political and social structure, area, demographic characteristics, climate and environmental conditions, resource endowments, and income levels.

It is thus not surprising to find that not all are affected equally, or in the same manner, by the agricultural crises which have just been outlined. Indeed, in studying this question one soon appreciates that there is not a single crisis, nor is there a single strategy to solve the problem.[1] On the contrary, there is sufficient diversity between countries that it is difficult to group the countries into manageable or consistent clusters within which a meaningful analysis and diagnosis can be conducted. Many countries share similar single attributes; the difficulty comes in finding correlations among the various attributes.

· ECONOMIC PARAMETERS ·

In terms of per head GNP, the World Bank currently classifies twenty-three of the countries as "low income," having a per head GDP of $400 or below in 1981 (converting at the official exchange rate). All the remainder, with the exception of Gabon, are classified as "lower middle-income" with a per head GNP of between $400 and $1700 in 1981. It is perhaps important to

Table 3.1 Structure of Sub-Saharan African Countries Classified by 1981 GNP in U.S. Dollars Per Head

Country	GNP Dollars	Growth rate Percentage Per Year 1960–81	Percentage Share of Agriculture in GDP 1982	Percentage of Labor Force in Agriculture 1980	Agriculture Forestry and Fishing as Percentage of Merchandise Exports 1981
Low Income (less than $300)					
Chad	110	–2.2	64	85	--
Ethiopia	140	1.4	49	80	91
Mali	190	1.3	43	73	--
Guinea-Bissau	190	na	54 [a]	83	--
Malawi	200	2.7	--	86	93
Zaire	210	–0.1	32	75	--
Uganda	220	–0.6	82	83	--
Burundi	230	2.4	56	84	--
Burkina Faso	240	1.1	41	82	85
Rwanda	250	1.7	46	91	--
Somalia	280	–0.2	60 [a]	82	94
United Republic of Tanzania	280	1.9	52	83	76
Low Income ($300–$400)					
Guinea	300	0.2	41	82	--
Benin	320	0.6	44	46	--
Central African Republic	320	0.4	35	88	74
Sierra Leone	320	(0.4)	32	65	--
Madagascar	330	–0.5	41	87	79
Niger	330	–1.6	31	91	17
Mozambique	na	na	--	66	--
Gambia	370	2.5	26	79	--
Sudan	380	–0.3	36	78	94
Togo	380	2.5	23	67	33
Ghana	400	–1.1	51	53	--
Lower Middle Income					
Kenya	420	2.9	33	78	52
Senegal	430	–0.3	22	77	29
Mauritania	460	1.5	29	69	--
Liberia	520	1.2	36	70	31
Lesotho	540	7.0	23	87	--
Zambia	600	0.0	14	67	--
Swaziland	760*	5.5	--	74	--
Angola	na*	na	--	59	--
Nigeria	870	3.5	22	54	--
Zimbabwe	870*	1.0	15 [a]	60	--
Cameroon	880	2.8	27 [a]	83	64
Botswana	1010*	7.9	21	78	--
Congo	1110	1.0	6	34	4
Côte–d'Ivoire	1200	2.3	26	79	82
Upper Middle Income					
Gabon	3810	4.9	7	77	--

-- data not available   *Oil exporter   [a]1979 data, Namibia excluded.

Source: GNP per head in dollars and percent growth rate—World Bank, *World Development Report 1983* (Washington, D.C.: World Bank, 1983), Table 1. Share of agriculture in GDP 1982—World Bank, *Toward Sustained Development*, Table 3. Percentage of labor force in agriculture 1980—World Bank, *Toward Sustained Development*, Table 27. Agriculture, forestry, and fishing as percentage of merchandise exports 1981—World Bank, *Toward Sustained Development*, Table 8.

stress again here the problems of data quality and the need for caution in interpreting GNP figures too literally. Nevertheless, within these overall low incomes the range is such that the countries with the highest incomes are many times better off than the countries with the lowest incomes (Table 3.1). As might be expected, the highest income countries are those that rely least on agriculture's contribution to GDP. In some countries the diversification comes mainly from the mining or extractive industries such as oil; in others it comes mainly from the manufacturing industry. However, even with its lower contribution to GDP, actual agricultural GDP per head in the high–income countries is substantially higher than agricultural GDP per head in the lowest income countries.

It is also apparent from Table 3.1 that there has been considerable variability in the growth of real GNP per head over the period 1960–1981. Nine countries have actually experienced a declining GNP per head over the past two decades, one of which (Senegal) is still in the lower middle–income category. At the other extreme Botswana (7.9 percent per year), Lesotho (7.0), Swaziland (5.5), Gabon (4.9), and Nigeria (3.5) have all experienced extremely rapid growth rates, due to mineral or oil extraction or links with the South African economy.

One generalization applied to sub-Saharan Africa is that it is agriculture dominated. This is undoubtedly true in terms of the proportion of the population engaged in agriculture since this exceeds 80 percent in eighteen countries and stands between 70 and 80 percent in ten others. However, there is a small group of countries whose proportion of the labor force in agriculture has fallen to 60 percent or below: Zimbabwe (60), Angola (59), Nigeria (54), Ghana (53), Benin (46), and the Congo (34) (Table 3.1). In most of these countries mineral and oil extraction is a major factor reducing the number engaged in agriculture.

The generally low productivity of agriculture means that the proportion of GDP accounted for by agriculture is substantially lower than its share of the labor force (Table 3.1). In 1982 the weighted average of agriculture's contribution to GDP in low–income countries was 50 percent, in middle-income oil importers 25 percent, and in middle-income oil exporters 21 percent. In only seven countries—Uganda (82), Chad (64), Somalia (60 in 1979), Burundi (56), Guinea-Bissau (54 in 1979), and the United Republic of Tanzania (52)—was the share above 50 percent. However, in thirteen countries the share was below 30 percent. These included two low- income countries, the Gambia (26) and Togo (23). Seven middle-income oil importing countries were also in this category, as were all of the oil exporters for which information is available. Thus in many sub-Saharan African countries it is no longer true to say that agriculture plays the dominant role in terms of contribution to GDP, but in most it is still an extremely important sector.

These two aspects of the role of agriculture, employment and contribution to GDP, together highlight the overall difference in average productivity (and frequently incomes) in the agricultural sector and the rest of the economy, particularly in those countries where the gap is widest. Perhaps the most extreme case is Gabon, where 77 percent of the population is described as agricultural but agriculture contributes only 7 percent of GDP.

• AGRICULTURAL SECTOR PERFORMANCE •

Total Agricultural Production

Again, although the performance of agriculture in general in terms of growth rate of total food and agricultural production has been described as disappointing, this disguises a wide range of performances in the individual countries. This is illustrated in Table 3.2, where countries are classified into four admittedly arbitrary groups according to their rate of growth of total agricultural production over the period 1969–1971 to 1979–1981. A fairly long time period and a three–year end period average have been used in an attempt to overcome the sensitivity of the results to year to year variability of production in some countries. Even so, some changes in the ranking could occur by altering the time period chosen.

This table shows that six countries have managed to maintain a growth rate of more than 3 percent per year over the past decade. On the other hand, fifteen countries had a recorded growth of less than 1 percent per year, including five countries whose total agricultural production was lower at the end of the 1970s than at the beginning of the decade. In many but by no means all of these countries there were major disruptions during the 1970s that undoubtedly contributed to the problem of maintaining agricultural growth. But there were other countries in the region experiencing disruptions during the decade that have maintained much better growth rates.

Total Food Production

Given the importance of food production in the agriculture of the region, it is not surprising to find a reasonably close relationship between agricultural and food production in most countries. However, only three countries had a growth rate of food production of more than 3 percent per year over this period while another thirteen had a growth rate of between 2 and 2.9 percent. Thus there were more countries with a "fair" performance and fewer

Table 3.2 Indicators of Agricultural Performance Percentage Per Annum 1969/71 to 1979/81. Countries ranked by rate of growth of total agricultural output.

	Rate of Growth of Total Production		Rate of Growth of Per Head Production		Differential Rate of Growth of Total Population and Agricultural Labor Force (1970–1980)	Agricultural Labor Productivity[a]	Rate of Growth of Agricultural Exports
	Agric. (1)	Food (2)	Agric. (3)	Food (4)	(5)	(6)	(7)
A. "Reasonable" performance							
Côte–d'Ivoire	4.6	5.2	0.5	1.0	1.3	1.6	19.0
Rwanda	3.7	3.4	0.7	0.4	0.8	1.5	18.0
Swaziland	3.7	3.1	1.0	0.5	1.7	2.9	19.7
Malawi	3.4	2.7	0.3	-0.4	1.1	1.4	16.1
Zimbabwe	3.2	2.6	-0.2	-0.8	1.6	1.4	19.0
Kenya	3.1	2.1	-0.7	-1.7	1.3	0.6	15.2
B. "Fair" performance							
Benin	2.4	2.5	-0.5	-0.4	1.5	1.0	3.7
Liberia	2.4	2.9	-1.1	-0.5	1.6	0.6	13.1
Cameroon	2.2	2.4	0	0.1	1.1	1.1	15.0
Nigeria	2.2	2.3	-1.0	-0.9	2.3	1.3	3.6
Zambia	2.2	2.2	-0.8	-0.8	1.6	0.7	1.2
Burundi	2.1	2.0	0.1	0	1.1	1.3	15.4
Central African Republic	2.1	2.3	-0.1	0.2	0.8	0.8	9.5
Niger	2.1	2.2	-0.8	-0.7	0.7	0	6.5
Burkina Faso	2.0	1.8	-0.4	-0.6	1.1	0.7	11.5
C. "Poor" performance							
Madagascar	1.9	1.9	-0.6	-0.6	1.3	0.8	10.9
Mali	1.7	1.3	-0.9	-1.3	0.9	0.1	21.2
United Republic of Tanzania	1.6	2.1	-1.4	-0.9	1.2	-0.2	7.8
Togo	1.6	1.7	-1.0	-1.0	1.5	0.4	9.5
Sudan	1.4	2.9	-1.2	0.2	1.0	-0.3	6.2
Chad	1.3	1.6	-0.7	-0.4	0.9	0.2	11.2
Zaire	1.2	1.3	-1.5	-1.4	1.3	-0.2	7.2
Guinea	1.1	1.0	-1.3	-1.4	1.2	-0.2	6.6
Namibia	1.0	0.9	-1.8	-1.9	2.0	0.3	13.0
D. "Very poor" performance							
Congo	0.6	0.5	-1.9	-2.0	2.5	0.6	5.1
Sierra Leone	0.6	0.5	-2.0	-2.1	1.6	-0.3	12.9
Somalia	0.6	0.6	-4.3	-4.3	0.7	-3.9	15.0
Ethiopia	0.5	0.5	-1.7	-1.7	1.1	-0.5	12.9
Guinea-Bissau	0.4	0.4	-1.2	-1.2	0.9	-0.1	11.2
Gabon	0.3	0.3	-0.6	-0.6	1.1	0.5	17.9
Lesotho	0.3	0.8	-2.0	-1.5	1.3	-0.7	10.2
Mauritania	0.2	0.2	-2.5	-2.5	0.8	-1.8	8.5
Senegal	0.1	0.1	-2.7	-2.7	1.4	-1.4	6.6
Ghana	0	0	-3.0	-3.9	2.0	-1.2	9.6
Uganda	-0.4	1.5	-3.4	-1.5	1.2	-2.2	4.9
Gambia	-1.0	-1.0	-3.9	-3.9	1.1	-2.8	5.4
Mozambique	-1.0	-0.7	-3.5	-3.1	2.0	-1.4	-1.1
Botswana	-1.7	-1.8	-4.3	-4.3	1.2	-3.2	18.9
Angola	-3.0	0	-5.2	-2.1	1.4	-3.9	-0.3

[a] Agricultural labor productivity is defined here as the difference in the percentage rate of growth per year in total agricultural production and the percentage rate of growth per year in the agricultural labor force.

Source: Columns 1–4 derived from FAO, *Production Yearbook 1981* (Rome: FAO, 1982), Tables 4–7. Columns 5–6 derived from FAO, *1983 Country Tables: Economics and Social Policy Department* (Rome: FAO, 1983). Column 7 derived from FAO Trade Yearbook.

with a "reasonable" or "poor" performance than in the case of agricultural production.

It is difficult to decide whether this pattern is an indication of peasant farmer rationality—i.e., that emphasis will be placed on food production initially and only when this is reasonably well satisfied will attention be directed to cash crop production—or whether this bunched performance is a statistical aberration. For instance, in many countries in the absence of actual information on subsistence production it is virtually assumed that food production will rise at or around the estimated rate of growth of the rural population.

Agricultural Exports

One might expect to find a reasonable correlation between agricultural output and agricultural export performance. This can operate in two ways. First, the higher the rate of growth of agricultural output, the more produce is available for export. Secondly, the higher the level of agricultural exports, the more foreign exchange earnings should be available to purchase necessary imported inputs to boost agricultural output. Column 7 of Table 3.2 shows the rate of growth of total agricultural and livestock exports in current dollar terms (this explains the overall high rates of growth). The "reasonable" performance countries do indeed show a uniformly high rate of growth of agricultural exports, which incidentally suggests that food crop production and agricultural exports do not necessarily conflict; but the other groups of countries show a more varied performance.

Per Head Agricultural and Food Production

Although the overall growth rate of agricultural and food production could be termed "reasonable" or "fair" in many countries, in no country did agricultural or food output per head grow at more than 1 percent per year over the 1970s. Indeed, in a large number of countries output growth failed to keep pace with population growth leading to a major feature of the crisis—falling food availability per head of population from domestic sources and declining agricultural production per head.

The result of deflating the rate of growth of total agricultural and food production by the population growth rate (Table 3.2, columns 3 and 4) is that only six countries show a positive rate of growth of agricultural production per head of population over the last decade, i.e., 1969–1971 to 1979–1981. Seven countries show a positive growth in food production per head of population, but most of the countries with a "fair," "poor," and "very poor" overall growth performance show a decline in agricultural and food production per head. In general a correlation between total production and per head production can be observed, but the effect of high population growth can be clearly seen in the case of Kenya and Zimbabwe, where "reasonable" total performance is associated with a negative rate of growth in per head terms.

Agricultural Labor Productivity

It is frequently assumed that this decline in production per head of population reflects a declining labor productivity within the agricultural sector. This is not necessarily so. While only six countries have a positive growth in agricultural production per head of population, twenty-two countries have a positive rate of growth of agricultural production per member of the economically active agricultural labor force over the period 1969–1971 to 1979–1981, and in another seven the fall in "agricultural labor productivity" was less than 0.5 percent per year (Table 3.2, column 6). The major reason for this difference is that the economically active agricultural labor force is growing much more slowly than the total population in most countries (see Tables 3.1 and 3.2). Two factors account for this: the current age structure of the population and the movement of labor out of agriculture. Another feature related to this is the very high dependency ratio. The economically active agricultural labor force represents less than 40 percent of the agricultural population and only around 25 percent of the total population of the region.

For some countries, this consideration sheds a rather different light on the performance of the agricultural sector. For instance, Nigeria is classified as having only a "fair" performance in terms of total agricultural output with an annual growth of 2.2 percent over the last decade. With an economically active agricultural labor force growing at only 0.9 percent per year, the implied rise in agricultural labor productivity was 1.3 percent per year (Table 3.2, column 6), which put Nigeria near the top of the "productivity league table" for the region. At the same time total population was rising at 3.2 percent per year, 2.3 percent per year faster than the agricultural labor force (Table 3.2, column 5). The increase in agricultural labor productivity covered only 1.3 percentage points of this gap, accounting for the dismal situation that agricultural production per head of population declined by 1 percent per year.

We can see, then, two types of situation in which countries managed to maintain agricultural output per head of population over the past decade. Some countries had a reasonable growth in agricultural labor productivity, and this was greater than the difference between the growth of total popula-

Table 3.3 Share of Total Cereal Imports, 1980–82

Nigeria	25.9
Côte–d'Ivoire	6.5
Senegal	5.4
Zaire	5.0
Sudan	4.5
Mozambique	4.3
Somalia	4.2
United Republic of Tanzania	4.2
	60.0

Source: FAO, *Trade Yearbook 1982.*

tion and the agricultural labor force. Most of the countries in the "reasonable" total performance group (Swaziland, Côte–d'Ivoire, Rwanda, Malawi) were in this position. Cameroon and the Central African Republic, in the "fair" total performance group, had a slightly lower productivity, but this was still sufficient to equal the gap between total population and agricultural labor force growth, leaving per head agricultural production unchanged. However, in countries like Zimbabwe and Nigeria, the relatively good increase in labor productivity was not sufficient to bridge the population-agricultural labor gap, and per head agricultural production fell. In all other countries the lower rates of productivity increase were insufficient to bridge the population-agricultural labor force gap. The "very poor" total performance group is characterized by considerable drops in agricultural labor productivity combined with the typical gap between the agricultural labor force and total population.

If countries wish to achieve higher levels of agricultural or food production per head of population, the solution seems to be in raising output per economically active member of the agricultural population to overcome the population-worker gap. If this led to higher real incomes for agricultural workers, it might also help to reduce rural-urban migration, which is at least part of the current problem.

Agricultural Imports

The dramatic rise in agricultural imports, and in particular the rise in cereal imports, is a feature of the agrarian crisis emphasized by many commentators. Even here, however, there are wide differences in the importance of cereal imports to different countries and substantial differences in the characteristics of the major importers. In terms of total cereal imports during 1980–1982, just eight countries accounted for 60 percent of the volume (Table 3.3). Not surprisingly Nigeria, with almost one quarter of the population, was the largest importer, with almost 26 percent of the subregion's imports. However, the second largest importer was the Côte–d'Ivoire, which with 2.4 percent of the population imported 6.5 percent of the cereals in volume terms. This may seem surprising, considering that the Côte–d'Ivoire is one of the few countries that have maintained a positive growth rate of agricultural and food production per head of population. On the other hand, the Côte–d'Ivoire is one of the more heavily urbanized countries in the region with a high rate of urban growth over the past decade and a relatively high and growing per head income. The demand for *marketed* cereals is therefore likely to be rising rapidly, and domestic marketed supply was adversely affected by changes in government pricing and procurement policies in the 1960s and 1970s.

When cereal imports are classified on a per head basis, the wide differences between countries become even more apparent (Table 3.4). In 1980–1982 there were ten countries with per head cereal imports of more than 50 kg per year, headed by Mauritania with an import of 110 kg per year. There was no single common factor linking all these countries, but six were in climatic zones where it is debatable whether cereal self-sufficiency is likely to be achieved and where it is extremely difficult to produce the "superior" cereals, wheat and rice. Only two of the ten would be classified by the World Bank as "low income" (the Gambia and Somalia), and Somalia is a special case because of its refugee population. The Gambia has traditionally oriented its agriculture toward export crops that have been used to pay for cereal imports, although the performance of groundnut exports from the

Table 3.4 Cereal Imports Per Head of Population, 1980–82 (kg)

More than 50 kg Per Head		25 to 49 kg Per Head		Less than 25 kg Per Head	
Mauritania	110	Congo	46	Niger	21
Lesotho	86	Angola	40	Sudan	20
Senegal	78	Guinea-Bissau	38	Togo	20
Botswana	76	Mozambique	34	Ghana	19
Somalia	73	Madagascar	29	United Republic	
Gambia	70	Nigeria	27	of Tanzania	19
Côte–d'Ivoire	66	Sierra Leone	27	Mali	15
Gabon	59	Guinea	26	Zaire	14
Zambia	54	Benin	26	Kenya	14
Liberia	52			Cameroon	14
				Burkina Faso	11
				Malawi	10
				Ethiopia	9
				Zimbabwe	8
				Central African	
				Republic	8
				Chad	6
				Burundi	4
				Uganda	4
				Rwanda	3

Source: FAO, *Trade Yearbook 1982.*

Gambia has been poor in recent years. Of the rest with most mining activities and fuels, minerals and metals constitute a significant or major part of merchandise exports. This tends to create a relatively high income enclave often remote from agricultural areas, which generates a demand that can frequently be most easily met by direct cereal imports.

Nine other countries imported more than 25 kg of cereals per head of population 1980–1982. Three of these, the Congo, Angola, and Nigeria, had relatively high incomes from oil and mineral mining activities. Incidentally, Nigeria, which because of its population accounts for 26 percent of the subregion's total cereal imports, imports only a modest 27 kg of cereals per head. The remaining countries are low income and import mainly wheat and rice. Most seem to have the potential to produce more cereals except wheat, and most might experience difficulty expanding their rice output. The remaining eighteen countries imported less than 25 kg of cereals per head in 1980–1982; fifteen of these are classified as low income. Thus, contrary to general belief, it is not the poorest countries in the region that are the major importers of cereals.

Food Availability

The availability of food supplies per head is, of course, a function of domestic food production and the level of food imports per head. As with all other aspects of the region, we find a wide spread of food supplies per head when measured in terms of the calorific food supply per head per day as a percentage of estimated requirements (Table 3.5). Given the tentative nature of food balance sheets for most countries in the region, there is probably a wide margin of error attached to these estimates. Nevertheless, the FAO estimates that in 1979–1980 twelve countries had a food supply of 100 percent or more of requirements, and a further five countries had a food supply equivalent to 95 percent or more of requirements. On the other hand, thirteen countries had a food supply equivalent to less than 90 percent of calorific requirements. There is thus no clear link between overall agricultural performance and calorie supplies per head.

There are both encouraging and disappointing features in this situation. The encouraging feature is that over the years a larger number of countries have raised their average calorific food supply above the 100 percent level, by increasing either domestic production or imports. In 1967 only four countries in the region were in this position; in 1970 there were five; in 1975 this had risen to eight; and in 1979–1980 to twelve. Of course, distribution of calorie supplies within these countries may be very uneven. On the other hand, the spread of food supplies among countries is now wider than previously, and a disappointing feature is that the food supply situation in all the twelve countries with the lowest percentage of requirements in 1979–1980 has deteriorated since 1967. In eight of these countries, food supplies generally since 1967 have represented 90 percent or less of calorific requirements. Chad was able to meet 100 percent of its calorific requirement in 1967, but there was a rapid decline up to 1975. Uganda was able to meet more than 90 percent of its requirements up to 1970 but has since declined below that level. In Ghana, Kenya, and Zambia the decline to below 90 percent of requirements has occurred since 1975.

• RESOURCE PARAMETERS •

Climatic Diversity[2]

Not surprisingly for a region as large as sub-Saharan Africa, there are a range of climatic and ecological zones influenced mainly by rainfall because

Table 3.5 Calorie Food Supply Per Head Per Day as Percentage of Requirement 1979–80 Average

Country	Percentage of Requirement	Country	Percentage of Requirement
"Reasonable" Total Performance		"Poor" Performance	
Côte–d'Ivoire	115	Madagascar	109
Rwanda	94	Mali	84
Swaziland	108	United Republic of Tanzania	86
Malawi	94	Togo	92
Zimbabwe	80	Sudan	102
Kenya	87	Chad	76
		Zaire	95
		Guinea	82
		Namibia	97
"Fair" Total Performance		"Very Poor" Performance	
Benin	101	Congo	100
Liberia	108	Sierra Leone	91
Cameroon	106	Somalia	93
Nigeria	99	Ethiopia	74
Zambia	86	Guinea-Bissau	101
Burundi	93	Gabon	122
Central African Republic	96	Lesotho	108
Niger	95	Mauritania	90
Burkina Faso	86	Senegal	101
		Ghana	87
		Uganda	79
		Gambia	95
		Mozambique	81
		Botswana	94
		Angola	89

Source: FAO, *Country Tables 1983* (Rome: World Bank, 1983).

temperature is generally high all the year.

The Sahel

In the Sahelian countries there are three major climatic zones. The northern areas of Mauritania, Mali, Niger, and Chad are hot tropical and subtropical desert. South of this, running east-west, is a semi-arid tropical belt sometimes called the Sahelo-Sudanese zone. This covers all of northern Senegal, much of southern Mauritania and Mali, northern Burkina Faso, and southern Niger and Chad. The average annual temperature is between 26 and 31 degrees centigrade and average annual rainfall between 400 and 1000 mm. The rainy season is short to very short (two to four months), and the high variability of rainfall makes drought an ever–present possibility. The dry season, with its harmattan wind, is extremely severe. Only highly drought-resistant crops can be grown, and it is only to the south of the zone that the climate becomes suitable for millet.

South of the Sahelo-Sudanese zone and again running east-west is the Sudano-Guinean zone, covering southern Senegal and the Gambia, and the southern parts of Mali, Burkina Faso, and Chad. Annual temperature averages between 24 and 28 degrees centigrade with between 950 and 1750 mm of rainfall spread over a five to seven month rainy season. This area is suited to millet, sorghum, and maize production.

West Africa

The Sudano-Guinean zone extends throughout most of the inland portions of Guinea-Bissau, Guinea, Sierra Leone, Liberia, Côte–d'Ivoire, Ghana, Togo, Benin, and central Nigeria. But the coastal strip of these countries, together with the Cameroon coast, lies in a belt of humid, semi-hot equatorial climate called the Guinean zone. In this latter zone the rainfall is bimodal and exceeds 1000 mm annually, reaching 2000 mm annually in Liberia. The dry season is very short, and temperatures at 25 to 27 degrees centigrade are relatively constant throughout the year. The Cameroon highlands, extending over much of the country, lie in the humid *tierra templada,* a monsoon-influenced climate warm enough for maize and suitable for coffee growing.

Central Africa

The Sudano-Guinean zone extends eastward across the major portion of the Central African Republic and the northern part of Zaire. Gabon, much of the Congo, and central Zaire are in the Guinean zone, sharing the same humid climate as the West African coast. Cassava is the staple best suited to these conditions. The uplands of southern Zaire and northern Angola are in the same climatic zone as the Cameroon highlands.

East Africa

The varying altitudes in East Africa have a considerable influence on the highly diverse climate. On the whole East Africa is much drier than the rest of Africa lying within the same latitudes. The effect of altitude is seen in the fact that the climatic zones tend to run north-south.

The coastal strip of Ethiopia, Djibouti, much of Somalia, Kenya, and the United Republic of Tanzania are in the relatively dry Sahelo-Sudanese zone together with much of the Sudan. A narrow coastal strip through northern Tanzania and southern Kenya has an abnormally high rainfall of approximately 2000 mm annually and can be classified as Guinean. The Rift Valley and the plateau south of Lake Victoria, which covers most of Rwanda, Burundi, and central Tanzania, are rather dry, but the high regions such as the Kenyan highlands and volcanoes and crests on either side of the Great Rift Valley are again in the humid *tierra templada* zone, receiving 1200 to 1500 mm of annual rainfall and suited to maize and coffee growing. The heights to the east of Lake Victoria and the Ethiopian highlands are cooler, being in the medium *tierra fria* zone.

Southern Africa

The high plateaux of southern Angola, Zambia, and Zimbabwe lie in the *tierra fria* zones well suited to maize production. Much of southern Mozambique lies in a low rainfall zone ranging from 200 to 600 mm with a cool winter. The northern plains are appreciably more humid and classified with the Guinean zone. Much of Namibia and southern Botswana are in the desert zones, with a tongue of monsoon subtropical zone stretching east-west across southern Angola and Zambia and northern Namibia and Botswana.

Food Systems

This diversity of climates also leads to a variety of basic staple foods being produced and consumed in different climatic areas. Recently the FAO has used this food consumption pattern to classify the countries of the region into six subgroups.

1. The Sudano-Sahel group of countries (Sudan, Senegal, Gambia, Niger, Burkina Faso, Mauritania, Mali, Chad), where millet and sorghum are the basic foods

2. Those where rice is the major component of the diet (Madagascar, Liberia, Guinea-Bissau, Sierra Leone, Guinea)

3. The main root–crop producing and consuming countries (the Congo, Zaire, the Central African Republic)

4. The group of countries in which grains and root crops are of equal importance (Gabon, Côte–d'Ivoire, Cameroon, Benin, Togo, Ghana)

5. The maize-producing and -consuming countries in eastern and southern Africa (Swaziland, Lesotho, Malawi, Botswana, Kenya, the United Republic of Tanzania, Zambia, Zimbabwe)

6. An additional group that does not fit easily into any of the above categories (Namibia, Rwanda, Burundi, Somalia, Angola, Mozambique, Uganda, Ethiopia)

Spatial Characteristics

Several countries in the region have a large land area and most have a low population density (Table 3.6). The Sudan, the largest country in terms of land area, is three-quarters the size of India but has less than 3 percent of India's population. Eleven other countries have a land area greater than

Table 3.6 Sub-Saharan African Countries: Land Area ('000 km^2) and Population Density (Persons Per km^2) in 1981

Country	Land Area	Population Density	Country	Land Area	Population Density
Sudan	2506	8	Zimbabwe	391	18
Zaire	2345	13	Congo	342	5
Chad	1284	4	Côte–d'Ivoire	322	26
Niger	1267	5	Burkina Faso	274	23
Angola	1247	6	Gabon	268	3
Mali	1240	6	Guinea	246	23
Ethiopia	1222	26	Ghana	239	49
Mauritania	1031	2	Uganda	236	55
United Republic			Senegal	196	30
of Tanzania	945	20	Malawi	118	53
Nigeria	924	95	Benin	113	32
Mozambique	802	16	Liberia	111	17
Zambia	753	8	Sierra Leone	72	50
Somalia	638	7	Togo	57	47
Contral African			Guinea-Bissau	36	22
Republic	623	4	Lesotho	30	47
Botswana	600	2	Burundi	28	150
Madagascar	587	15	Rwanda	26	204
Kenya	583	30	Swaziland	17	35
Cameroon	475	18	Gambia	11	55
(Namibia excluded)					

Source: World Bank, *World Development Report 1983* (Washington, D.C.: World Bank, 1983), Table 1.

France and West Germany's combined area of 800 thousand km². Most countries have a very low population density; the only countries approaching the population density of, say, India (210 persons per km²) are Burundi (150) and Rwanda (204).

While this aspect of land area and population density is useful in considering problems of infrastructure provision and explaining some of the difficulties of servicing rural areas adequately, it can be misleading when considering the actual or potential availability of land for agricultural purposes due to severe climatic and environmental limitations on land use in some parts of the subregion. For instance, Niger, one of the countries with the lowest population density per unit of land area, has only two hectares of arable land per head of population, and 96 percent of the rainfed area is already in use. Table 3.7 shows that twelve countries already have less than one hectare of available arable land per head of population, while six countries are extremely well endowed with more than five hectares of available arable land per head of population. In these countries the vast majority of rainfed land was not in use in 1975.

Demographic Features

The countries of the subregion also vary widely in terms of population size (Table 3.8). Many of the countries are extremely small; fifteen of the thirty-nine (and the six excluded from examination) had populations of less than five million in 1981. Another twelve had populations of between five and ten million.

The combination of low per capita GNP and small populations means that many of these countries are extremely small economic entities. They thus find it difficult to establish certain types of infrastructure, such as research capability and universities, on an individual country basis. As the Berg report points out, the whole of sub-Saharan Africa, with a population of 380 million, has a GDP only one-third greater than that of the Netherlands, with a population of fourteen million.[3]

On the other hand, some countries have large populations. Nigeria (87.6 million) and Ethiopia (32.0 million) have a combined population greater than that of the twenty-seven countries with less than ten million. These two countries, together with Zaire, Sudan, and the United Republic of Tanzania, contain over half the population of the entire subregion. This skewed distribution leads to considerable difficulties when analyzing the results of groups of countries; e.g., any analysis of the West African area is completely dominated by the presence of Nigeria.

Although population growth for the entire subregion was around 2.8 percent, for individual countries population growth rates over the period

Table 3.7 Sub-Saharan African Countries Classified by Total Available Arable Land Per Head of Population 1981

Country	Arable Land Per Head of Population 1981	Rainfed Area in Use Percentage Total Available Rainfed Area 1975	Cropping Intensity Percentage 1975
More than 5 Hectares Arable Land Per Head			
Congo	12.5	3	32
Gabon	12.1	4	31
Central African Republic	11.6	21	15
Zambia	9.0	10	30
Angola	8.0	7	37
Zaire	5.1	9	36
1–5 Hectares Arable Land Per Head			
Chad	3.8	40	24
Sudan	3.2	21	46
Madagascar	3.1	7	75
Cameroon	2.9	29	43
Zimbabwe	2.5	13	56
Mozambique	2.5	16	54
Niger	2.0	96	37
Mali	2.0	82	16
Liberia	2.0	36	33
Senegal	1.7	53	46
United Republic of Tanzania	1.7	20	74
Benin	1.6	51	30
Côte–d'Ivoire	1.5	70	37
Burkina Faso	1.3	83	45
Guinea	1.2	61	35
Mauritania	1.0	46	23
Less than 1 Hectare Arable Land Per Head			
Gambia	0.8	73	51
Ghana	0.8	47	82
Togo	0.7	96	32
Ethiopia	0.7	60	54
Uganda	0.7	60	82
Malawi	0.6	62	86
Sierra Leone	0.6	85	45
Nigeria	0.5	76	76
Somalia	0.4	55	60
Kenya	0.4	59	78
Burundi	0.3	84	96
Rwanda	0.2	91	95

Source: FAO, *Agriculture Towards 2000* (Rome: FAO, 1981).

1967–1981 ranged from only 0.9 percent per year in Gabon to Somalia's exceptional 4.6 percent per year caused by the flow of refugees (Table 3.3). Population pressure thus had much more influence on production per head in some countries than in others.

Table 3.8 Sub-Saharan African Countries Classified by Population (Millions), Mid-1981

Less than 2 Million		5–9.9 Million		10–19.9 Million	
Gambia	0.6	Guinea	5.6	Ghana	11.8
Swaziland	0.6	Niger	5.7	Mozambique	12.5
Gabon	0.7	Zambia	5.8	Uganda	13.0
Guinea-Bissau	0.8	Senegal	5.9	Kenya	17.4
Lesotho	1.4	Malawi	6.2	United Republic	
Mauritania	1.6	Burkina Faso	6.3	of Tanzania	19.1
Congo	1.7	Mali	6.9	Sudan	19.2
Liberia	1.9	Zimbabwe	7.2	Subtotal	93.0
Subtotal	9.3	Angola	7.8		
		Côte–d'Ivoire	8.5	20 Million+	
2–4.9 Million		Cameroon	8.7	Zaire	29.8
Central African		Madagascar	9.0	Ethiopia	32.0
Republic	2.4	Subtotal	83.6	Nigeria	87.6
Togo	2.7			Subtotal	149.4
Benin	3.6				
Sierra Leone	3.6			TOTAL	360.7
Burundi	4.2				
Somalia	4.4				
Chad	4.5				
Subtotal	25.4				

Source: World Bank, *World Development Report 1983* (Washington, D.C.: World Bank, 1983), Table 1.

• SUMMARY •

When the economic characteristics of the agricultural sector performance and resource parameters are considered, there is no such thing as a "typical" African country. Indeed, some of the evidence presented here will be used in the next chapter to refute some of the sweeping generalizations used to explain the agricultural crisis.

But even if we are dealing with a large number of heterogeneous countries, there are some useful lessons that can be learned from the evidence. Despite the overall poor performance, some countries in the region in various climatic zones have maintained a reasonable agricultural growth rate over the past decade, and some useful lessons might be learned from studying these in more depth. They include several countries whose population pressure on the available arable land is intense. This suggests that it is possible, at least in some climatic zones, to find productive farming systems and technologies suited to high population pressures. Even some of the Sahelian countries have achieved a "fair" performance over the decade of the 1970s.

The evidence also suggests that there is no necessary conflict between increasing food production and expanding agricultural exports. Conversely, a poor agricultural performance does not necessarily mean an overall food shortage since several countries have had the facility to import food supplies. Of course, this does not deny the fact that a better agricultural performance could avoid foreign exchange earnings being devoted to food. Moreover, an improved agricultural performance could raise the real living standards of the rural population.

The gap between total population growth and agricultural labor force growth seems to be both a cause and a symptom of the crisis. The solution must be found in improved agricultural labor productivity and rewards. A major question to be resolved is how this can be achieved. In particular, many of the countries are so small in terms of population and GDP that it is difficult to envisage them supporting an effective research organization without regional cooperation or international collaboration.

• NOTES •

1. This is a point stressed by FAO, *Regional Food Plan for Africa* (Rome: FAO, 1980).

2. This section draws heavily on USDA, *Food Problems and Prospects in Sub-Saharan Africa: The Decade of the 1980s,* ERS, Foreign Agricultural Research Report No. 1966 (Washington, D.C., 1981), pp. 57–60.

3. World Bank, *Accelerated Development in Sub-Saharan Africa: An Agenda for Action* (The Berg Report) (Washington, D.C., 1981), pp. 57–60.

·4·

Causes of the Crisis

F rom the evidence presented in the preceding chapters, it is clear that while there are many facets of the agricultural crisis confronting African countries, the most worrying aspect is low and declining rates of growth of agricultural output. Furthermore, the crisis was shown to be of a long-term nature and, despite considerable diversity in country performances, it affected a large number of countries. As shown in Chapter 3, only five countries attained a positive rate of growth of per head agricultural production between 1969–1971 and 1979–1981.

In this chapter, we examine the various hypotheses that have been advanced to explain this crisis. This is not an easy task since, despite an outpouring of publications on the subject, few researchers have systematically addressed themselves to this issue. More often they have been content to reproduce a more or less long list of causes that are alleged to be responsible for the crisis. Few attempts have been made to assess the relative importance of different causes or to see them as a part of a dynamic, interactive process.

The lack of a rigorous, widely accepted explanation of the crisis is hardly surprising. The data are neither adequate nor reliable enough to permit the testing of alternative hypotheses. Some systemic explanations of the crisis are so broad and complex that they do not lend themselves to verification by conventional methods. Differences in language and modes of analysis of different researchers often exaggerate the divergence among them. Indeed, at times such apparent differences may mask essential points of agreement. Perhaps most important given the enormous differences among countries with respect to resources, structures, and policies, there is likely to be a different pattern of factors behind the crisis in each country. Any general explanation covering the entire region will inevitably skate over these differences.

The purpose of this chapter is not to offer a new hypothesis on the African agricultural crisis but to review in a somewhat systematic manner the

39

alternative explanations that have been advanced. Wherever possible we assess the validity of these explanations in the light of empirical evidence or theoretical analysis. We review successively the hypotheses ascribing the crisis to the colonial heritage, the operation of the world economic system, inappropriate or backward technology, population growth, environmental degradation, climatic changes, political instability, overall mismanagement and inefficiency, and a series of specific policies discriminating against agriculture. These include low agricultural prices, inadequate expenditure on agricultural programs and neglect of rural infrastructure. Most analysts ascribe the crisis to a multiplicity of factors. It may nevertheless be useful for analytical purposes to discuss these separately.

• COLONIAL HERITAGE •

A common theme throughout much of the literature is that the basis of the current agricultural crisis can be traced to the colonial era. There are many versions of what might be termed the "colonial hypothesis."[1] It is most generally argued that colonialism sowed the seeds of recurrent and deepening crisis by introducing or extending the exchange economy, foreign investment, and market integration with the capitalist world. We shall have occasion to revert to this argument in the next section. In more concrete terms, there are at least four ways in which colonialism is alleged to have contributed to the current crisis. The first two relate to its profound impact on the pattern and structure of agricultural production. The third and fourth relate to the charges that colonial administrations neglected rural infrastructure and education and training of skilled manpower. A full discussion of these issues is beyond the scope of this work, but a few words on each are in order.

Cash Crops Versus Food Products

Colonial administrations introduced or greatly stimulated the production of cash crops throughout the region. For the most part this amounted to the cultivation of export crops for sale in developed countries. Cash crops made possible the collection of a variety of taxes from peasants, and they brought in foreign exchange. In addition, they were considered the sole or the most efficient way of increasing the standard of living of the peasantry. The critics of this policy argue that by concentrating the resources on export crops, the colonial governments deprived the food sector of good land, labor and capital, thus laying the foundations for the contemporary food crisis.

There is no denying the neglect of food production, especially the indigenous crops, during the colonial period in most African countries. The lack of research, credit, extension services, and marketing for the food sector perpetuated low productivity and antiquated techniques of production. In that sense, the colonial agricultural policies share the blame for the food problems of the past decade or so. In defense of the colonial emphasis on cash crops, it must be stated that because of the lack of a sizeable market for food crops, especially the indigenous ones, the cultivation of export crops appeared to be the most efficient and quickest way of generating revenue for the state and cash incomes for the growers. Furthermore, through much of the colonial period, food was not the problem it has become since the 1970s. This is not to deny the occurrence of periodic famines and food shortages or the more enduring problems of malnutrition and undernutrition, but the "modern" food problem in Africa is a product of forces that emerged on the national scene in a subsequent period. Finally, it is by no means clear that food and cash crop production are always competing activities. There are no doubt situations in which land scarcity and coincidence of peak labor demands can have adverse effects on food production, but the opposite situation is quite common when the improved management and cultivation practices, use of inputs such as fertilizer and pesticides, and general technical progress spill over from cash crop to food production. It must be remembered that in Africa a typical peasant will grow both food and cash crops on the same plot.

Certainly the evidence presented in Chapter 3 suggests that a large majority of the countries with the highest rates of growth in total food production in the 1970s, over 2.5 percent per year, also had extremely high rates of growth of exports. There are, of course, several countries whose poor food performance is associated with a high rate of growth of agricultural exports; Mali is perhaps the classic example of this. This may be due in part to a competition between export and food crops for available labor time in peak seasons. But there are even more countries with both a poor food and export performance. The weight of the empirical evidence thus cannot support the view that the food crisis is the result of the encouragement of export crop production. It is more appropriate to regard the crisis as embracing the entire agricultural sector rather than food production alone.

Dualism and the Crisis

The colonial powers altered not only the patterns but also the structures of agricultural production. It is argued that the introduction of new modes of production, especially of plantations and large settler-owned farms, created dualistic structures in the agricultural sectors of many African countries. This dualism is alleged to have contributed to the agricultural crisis through a drain of resources from the peasant to the large farm sector and concentration of public resources on the latter. It should first be noted that this argument applies in its full force only to some countries in eastern and southern Africa. There is no doubt that historically the peasant farmer was subjected to a series of discriminatory practices in the settler- and plantation-dominated economies in several east, central, and southern African countries.[2] This naturally had a debilitating effect on the vitality and dynamism of this sector. But in most cases these trends were reversed before or soon after independence, although it must be admitted that in many countries the predilection in favor of the large farm sector has persisted, and it continues to receive the lion's share of the limited resources of credit and expertise. But, on the other side, it should be stated that precisely because of settler and plantation dominance, the agricultural sector generally received more official resources during the colonial period in countries such as Kenya, Nyasaland and Northern and Southern Rhodesia (as they were called then) than might have been the case otherwise. Also, as shown in Chapter 7, the settler pressure was successful in bending government pricing, marketing, and rural infrastructure development policies in its favor. While weakening the peasant sector, the plantations and large farms at the same time provided a dynamic element in the agricultural sector that often contributed powerfully to the diversification and growth of output.

Neglect of Human and Physical Infrastructure

Another criticism of the colonial era was the lack of a basic infrastructure, which in some areas was almost nonexistent. Roads, railways, ports, and communications systems were scant and did not penetrate the hinterland. Public capital investment was limited by both the shortage of local resources and the doctrine of colonial self-sufficiency that prevailed until World War II. The failure, or the inability, to provide sufficient investment for transport systems since independence is now a major factor hindering agricultural development in many countries.

The colonial authorities also failed abysmally in training manpower, and it has been argued that this has been one of the most critical problems hampering the development process in the past twenty years.[3] This has been caused partially by a failure to extend advanced education to the African population, a reliance on immigrants for skilled work, and a reluctance to allow Africans to supervise non-Africans, thus preventing them from moving up the skill ladder or assuming entrepreneurial roles.

When the colonial authorities belatedly turned their attention to encouraging African agriculture, there was a tendency to favor particular areas or individuals, especially those who had cooperated with the colonial authorities. Many countries introduced a "master farmer" approach, channeling extension, resources, and credit to a limited number of farmers who frequently, because of their position, already owned more resources than the average farmer. This approach is still in vogue in many countries. Although many farmers responded well to this encouragement, this elitist approach undoubtedly sharpened inequalities among both individuals and districts; such inequalities have persisted over time. This policy might have been justified if it had been a means of economizing on scarce resources and a "demonstration effect" was expected to lead to a rapid uptake of innovations by all farmers. In practice, however, the innovations were frequently inappropriate for resource-poor farmers, and the failure of the "trickle down" approach in these circumstances was often mistaken for indolence and laziness, which reinforced the tendency to concentrate on the "progressive" (i.e., resource-rich) farmers.

It is undoubtedly true that colonial attitudes and neglect created severe problems for newly independent nations, but most countries have now been independent for too long to continue to lay all the blame for the failure of the agricultural sector on the colonial authorities. As will be argued later, several governments chose to give very low priority to the agricultural sector or have mismanaged its development. In addition, for many of the resource-poor countries, the task of developing an adequate transport, marketing, and research capacity sufficient to raise agricultural productivity and food output dramatically has proved impossible with the physical and human resources available.

• INTEGRATION IN THE WORLD ECONOMIC SYSTEM •

Some argue that the crisis in Africa is inextricably linked with its integration in the world economic system.[4] This argument is closely related to the colonial hypothesis in that it was colonialism that was responsible for linking the periphery to the center through flows of trade, capital, technology, and people. There are many variants of this argument, but most proponents would subscribe to the statement that in the relationship between industrialized capitalist countries and backward economies there are forces that work systematically to the advantage of the former and the impoverishment of the latter.

To elaborate the argument further, it is alleged that the trade relationship between rich and poor countries is characterized by unequal exchange, which results in disadvantageous and steadily deteriorating terms of trade for primary product exporting countries. Likewise, proponents of the argument allege that foreign investment through multinational corporations drains the surplus from these countries. Foreign technology, management and know-how extract monopoly returns for their services and further deepen the dependence of poor countries on the developed world. The integration in the world economy distorts the economies of underdeveloped countries, resulting in vast inequalities and structural disequilibrium in patterns of production, demand, and consumption. The surplus generated is either transferred abroad, dissipated in unproductive luxury consumption, or invested to serve the interests of a tiny affluent minority. This model is said to be particularly applicable to sub-Saharan Africa, with its extreme dependence on primary product exports to industrialized countries and on imports of capital, technology, and know-how.

Anyone familiar with the workings of African economies will recognize the important insights contributed by this school of thought to the elucidation of the African crisis. While there continues to be controversy about the long-run trend in the terms of trade of primary producers, there is general agreement that these have generally been unfavorable since the early 1970s. The slow-down of growth in the industrialized world since 1973 and particularly the severe recession of 1980–1982 have had a strong negative effect on the export earnings and economies of most African countries. This period also witnessed the two oil shocks of 1973–1974 and 1980, which further buffeted the oil-importing African countries.

Despite the validity of many of the arguments presented above, it is difficult to believe that the African crisis is entirely or largely of external origin and that domestic policies and factors have played a minor or negligible role. Indeed, the school of thought reviewed here does not make this claim. It argues rather that the national bourgeoisie, in cooperation with foreign capital, is responsible for policies that are at the heart of the crisis. The validity of the argument that ascribes the crisis to the working of the world economic system is also called into question by more favorable experiences of several countries in Africa and other developing regions. Indeed, there does not seem to be any correlation between performance and depth of integration in the world economy. What appears more important is an organized national effort to take advantage of the opportunities afforded by the world economic system. Unfortunately, the lower the national capability and discipline and the more corrupt the social and economic system, the less the country is likely to benefit from external integration.

• TECHNOLOGICAL BACKWARDNESS AND INAPPROPRIATE TECHNOLOGY •

The technological backwardness of African agriculture is increasingly cited as a major cause of the agricultural crisis.[5] Yields of most crops on both a per hectare and per work-hour basis are low by international standards. This may reflect differences in underlying potential (ecological conditions), backward production techniques, differences in scale, effectiveness of research efforts, or some combination of each. Most food production occurs on small farms by cultivators working with simple hand tools. Fertilizer consumption, the use of mechanization, and irrigation in Africa all lag seriously behind the levels in other developing regions (Table 4.1). Technical progress in improving staple food crops has been limited. In part this is a reflection of the neglect of food production in colonial times, but there are several other factors constraining improvements. Most production is predominantly rainfed, which means that most of the new cereal varieties developed for irrigated agriculture in Asia cannot be transferred to sub-Saharan Africa. Location-specific factors such as soil type, amount and length of the rainfall periods, altitude, and diseases have limited the transfer of improved varieties from other areas within the region. Local research efforts have been constrained by lack of experienced personnel, inadequate funding, and poor integration with existing farming practices. Insufficient attention has been paid to the complexity of farming systems and in particular to the fact that most existing farming practices are extremely labor-intensive, with the result that labor, not land, is frequently the limiting factor of production. This labor shortage problem is exacerbated, or perhaps created, by the limited rainfall periods in most of the region that lead to peak labor requirements for soil preparation and planting, weeding, and harvesting opera-

Table 4.1 Indicators of Agricultural Resources and Technology

Country Group	Fertilizer Consumption Per Hectare of Cultivated Area		Proportion of Cultivated Area Which is Irrigated		Number of Tractors Per 1000 Hectares Cultivated Area	
	Average 1978–80 (kg)	Average Annual Rate of Change 1971–80 (percent)	Average 1978–80 (percent)	Average Annual Rate of Change 1971–80 (percent)	Average 1978–80 (number)	Average Annual Rate of Change 1971–80 (percent)
Developing Market Economies						
Africa	8.2	4.5	1.7	2.7	1.4	2.2
Far East	35.1	9.4	24.8	1.9	2.0	10.5
Latin America	42.2	8.6	8.6	2.3	5.4	2.3
Near East	33.0	10.0	21.4	1.0	6.6	13.3
Asian Centrally Planned Economies	128.3	14.7	43.2	1.6	6.4	16.8
All Developing Countries	44.5	10.8	19.2	1.5	3.7	8.4
All Developed Countries	115.9	3.3	8.7	3.1	26.6	2.3

Source: FAO, *Socio-economic Indicators Relating to Agricultural Sector and Rural Development 1984* (Rome: FAO, 1984), Tables 11, 7, 9.

tions. Many of the innovations suggested by research stations are frequently inappropriate for low-resource farmers with limited access to additional sources of mechanization and labor. Most new technologies still aim to increase the productivity of land with little regard for improving labor productivity. Research infrastructure in general is limited, and in many of the smaller, poorer countries there is not a sufficient critical mass to make research into topics such as disease control economically worthwhile.

At the same time, agricultural extension services, which have been a major instrument for rural development in Africa, have suffered the organizational weaknesses characteristic of almost all public sector agencies. But these are aggravated by special problems such as the distance from urban centers, which hampers recruitment of capable managers and middle-level technicians; a shortage of operating funds, which immobilizes staff and undermines morale; a dearth of women extension officers even though a high proportion of rural households is female-headed and many agricultural decisions and operations are undertaken by women. Most important, however, is the failure of the research stations to generate new and appropriate technological packages so that in many instances the extension staff do not have a valid message to extend. This does not apply to all crops and regions—hybrid maize has been extremely successful in Kenya—but the available technological packages are generally weak for traditional food crops and are especially uncertain for the climatically harsher regions. A recent review[6] of the evidence in different ecological zones of sub-Saharan Africa supports the contention that research has been neglected in the past and that much of the research that has been conducted is not appropriate for resource-poor farmers.

It may be argued that many of these factors have been present for a long time and thus their relevance in explaining the deterioration in performance is not obvious. There are, however, two new elements that may have contributed to the crisis. First, in many countries the research stations and the extension services have suffered a marked decline in quality and quantity in recent years. Secondly, as argued in the next section, in a situation of fixity of land but rapid population growth the marginal returns to labor and soil fertility are likely to decline unless offset by technological progress. This technological progress has not been forthcoming in most African countries.

• POPULATION PRESSURE, ENVIRONMENT AND CLIMATE •

One noticeable feature of the sub-Saharan region over the past two decades has been the high and rising population growth rate, caused by a large reduction in the death rate unmatched as yet by a declining birth rate. The rate of population growth in this region has risen from 2.4 percent per year in the 1960s to 2.8 percent in the 1970s and probably to over 3 percent in the 1980s, making it the region with the highest population growth rate in the world. Although death rates are still the highest in the world and life expectancy the lowest, over the past two decades life expectancy has increased from 38 to 45 per thousand.

The population increase obviously has an impact on the demand for food and calls for a high and sustained rate of growth of food production if it is to be met from domestic sources. A limited number of countries in the region (and many others in other regions) have been able to meet this challenge in the past decade (see Table 3.2, column 4). But it has also had an effect on the farming systems in many areas. In large areas of the region, population pressure until recently was sufficiently low that some form of shifting cultivation has been practiced. Land was cultivated for a few years until its fertility declined when a new area would be opened up instead, the original area being left for perhaps as long as twenty to thirty years before it was necessary to return there. Table 3.8 shows that in 1975 sixteen countries still used less than 50 percent of their rainfed area.

Increasing population pressure inevitably reduces the length of the fallow period, prevents regeneration of mature vegetation, and eventually will lead to a reduction in soil fertility and labor productivity unless there is some change in the underlying agricultural technology and farming system. Eventually a stage may be reached where population density prevents shifting cultivation and all the available land within a certain area is permanently settled. In the process the failure of the vegetative cover to regenerate and the increasing demands for wood and fuel and building lead to deforestation; this in turn may accelerate soil erosion and the loss of soil fertility. At this stage, or even earlier, the increasing population will encourage people to migrate to areas of lower population density where land is more readily available. In many circumstances this entails a movement into areas of lower and more variable rainfall, where people are more at risk from climatic variability and crop failure unless farming systems can be introduced that are well adapted to the new environment. These processes are widespread in Africa and have been well documented. While the more spectacular examples of Ethiopia and the Sahelian countries have captured the world headlines, in varying degrees these processes are at work in most African countries with deleterious effects on agricultural productivity and yields.[7]

Although the threat of environmental degradation is serious, it must be remembered that concern with soil erosion was a common feature of agricultural officers' reports in the colonial era and even earlier. It does not necessarily follow that increased population pressure will inevitably lead to erosion. Farming systems can be adapted and farmers can be taught the benefits of soil conservation. As shown in Chapter 3, some of the more successful countries in terms of growth rate of total agricultural production have been those with the highest population density per hectare of arable land, such as Rwanda, Malawi, and Kenya.

Some people would argue that this change in vegetation within Africa is itself influencing the climate, but at this stage it is difficult to establish the validity of this. There is also considerable speculation that a global warming trend due to the build-up of atmospheric carbon dioxide leading to the "greenhouse effect" is under way, but this has yet to be substantiated. As indicated earlier, droughts are not a new phenomenon in sub-Saharan Africa, and if one considers a very long time period, droughts seem not to be more frequent or more severe than they were in the past. Nevertheless, the occurrence of severe drought in the Sahelian countries in the early 1970s and in these and eastern and southern African countries in the early 1980s contributed significantly to poor agricultural performance. However, it would be more appropriate to regard their role as triggering off the famines in situations in which a variety of other forces have combined to bring about the agricultural crisis.

• POLITICAL INSTABILITY, ECONOMIC MISMANAGEMENT AND INEFFICIENCY •

So far we have discussed the contribution of external and exogenous factors to the origin and intensification of the agricultural crisis in Africa. In this and the next section we turn to the so-called internal factors. These include political instability, economic management, and policies towards agriculture. Although we have followed the conventional practice in this classification, in truth the internal factors are also subject to a variety of external influences ranging from the prodding of aid agencies and pressures by dominant powers to alliances between domestic groups and foreign investors and financiers.

Political Instability

Sub-Saharan Africa has been racked by political crisis and instability over the past two decades. The crisis has been provoked by domestic unrest, conflicts with the neighboring states, and, in the southern African context, by the struggles for national liberation and aggression by the regime in South Africa. In the process a large number of countries have been affected by unrest and violence. To take only the more prominent cases, Chad, Sudan, Ethiopia, and Uganda have been ravaged by civil war for extended periods. Somalia, Ethiopia, Uganda, the United Republic of Tanzania, and Mauritania have been involved in border wars. Zimbabwe, Mozambique, and Angola waged prolonged liberation wars, have all suffered aggression from South

Africa, and the last two are still engaged in civil wars with extensive involvement by foreign powers. A number of countries, among them Ghana and Nigeria, have suffered from continuing political instability resulting in frequent coups and changes in administration. A tragic indicator of the continuing turbulence is the existence of an estimated ten million refugees in sub-Saharan Africa.

Political instability naturally has a strongly negative impact on economic growth. Not only are the limited financial and human resources diverted to military purposes but lack of security for life and property disrupts normal production and reduces productive investment. It is, therefore, not surprising to find countries that have been involved in prolonged conflicts among the worst economic performers in the region.

It would be a mistake to regard the political instability in the region as fortuitous or exogenous. While inherited ethnic tensions and border disputes have been important in a number of cases, there is also the problem of the legitimacy of political institutions and leadership. The latter in turn has been caused at least in part by the behavior of the ruling circles in some countries and the continuing economic crisis induced by mismanagement and inefficiency.

Economic Mismanagement and Inefficiency

Here we consider the argument relating to the overall management of the economy, leaving to the next section the discussion of policies towards the agricultural sector. A large number of commentators of widely divergent ideological backgrounds have blamed overall mismanagement for economic stagnation in general and the agricultural crisis in particular.[8] There are many different versions of this argument, but for convenience the various charges can be classified under two main headings. The first type may be described as unrequited transfers or appropriation of resources, while the second type refers to inefficiency in terms of inappropriate development strategies and policies, wrong choice of development projects and programs and suboptimal use of scarce resources.

The first type covers a wide range of malpractices, including kickbacks on contracts, commissions on import or foreign exchange licenses, smuggling of goods, illegal transfers of prohibited articles, outright theft of public property, raids on national exchequers, payments for goods never delivered, and nonrepayment of loans and credits from financial institutions. An essential feature of such malpractices is that they constitute payments to individuals and corporate groups in exchange not for goods and services but for favors rendered by virtue of political or official position. They are therefore in the nature of transfers or grants for unproductive and parasitic behavior, and their payment constitutes a burden on the productive members of the society with adverse effects on their savings, investment, and work efforts. In addition, widespread occurrence of such practices diverts national energies and talents to activities that do not generate real production or wealth. However, in situations of excessive bureaucratic regulation of the economy, these may serve to quicken decision-making and lubricate the creaking wheels of the economy.

The media reports, the commissions of inquiry, the court cases, and the gossip from reliable sources that circulate freely in the capitols all testify to the widespread occurrence of such practices in most African countries— indeed, in most developing countries. But by their very nature, it is not possible to quantify their dimensions nor assess even roughly the magnitude of their adverse impact on economic growth.

Writings by economists have generally singled out inappropriate economic policies as the core element in the crisis.[9] The litany of charges is quite extensive, but a few key points will suffice. It is argued that the macropolicy framework has led to distortions in resource allocation. The most common distortions mentioned are that wages for unskilled workers are too high and the real price of capital is too low, encouraging excessive capital intensity in industrial production. The exchange rate is overvalued so that the prices of tradeable goods—exports and imports—are too low in relation to those of other goods. This leads to recurrent shortages of foreign exchange with adverse effects on the entire economy. Through a variety of means, the prices of agricultural goods are held low in relation to other goods and services, a charge which will be examined in the next section.

Another type of inefficiency is said to arise from wrong investment decisions. It is argued that investment in industry and prestigious urban construction projects has taken up too large a proportion of resources in relation to agriculture. Investment decisions have favored large, capital-intensive projects while the need is for smaller, decentralized activities. The system of organizing production and the mechanisms used to regulate economic activity have also come in for a great deal of criticism. It is argued that there has been a proliferation of unproductive bureaucracies and of loss-making, inefficient state enterprises in agriculture, industry, commerce, construction, and marketing. The regulation of the economy by markets has been increasingly replaced by centralized decision-making, quantitative restrictions, licenses, and price-fixing by governmental agencies.

There is no doubt that over the last two decades there has been a steady movement towards *dirigism* in practically all African countries. Furthermore, the tendencies towards certain biases in macropolicies and investment decisions have also been evident in an increasing number of countries, although the situation is less clear-cut than is often implied and exigencies for the adoption of some of these policies more stringent than is generally recognized.

There can be little doubt that wrong macropolicies, investment decisions, and regulating mechanisms can inflict severe damage on an economy. This can take the form of reducing output below the normal capacity of the economy, diverting resources into less productive activities, lowering the investment potential, and blunting incentives to save, accumulate, and work. It is debatable to what extent wrong economic policies and institutions have contributed to the crisis in relation to other factors reviewed in this chapter, but there can be little doubt that in some countries wrong economic policies have been critical and in most they have made some contribution to the crisis.

• DISCRIMINATION AGAINST THE RURAL SECTOR •

This is a variant of the more general argument presented in the preceding section. The essence of the argument is that for a variety of reasons the governments in most African countries have discriminated against the rural sector.[10] This discrimination has taken various forms, including low prices for agricultural products, limited availability of public social and economic services in rural areas, and a relatively small proportion of investment funds for rural development projects.

The point made most frequently is that the real prices of agricultural goods have been depressed by a variety of policies.[11] Since the second part of this study is devoted to agricultural prices, the discussion here will be relatively brief. It is argued that the governments move the terms of trade against farmers because they wish to encourage industrialization, raise public revenue, and keep food prices low in urban areas. This in turn is possible because, despite the large majority constituted by peasants in all African countries, they are unable, because of lack of organization, to exert political power to bend policies in their favor. The government is able to buy the support of specific segments of the rural society such as large farmers, plantation owners, and progressive smallholders through special schemes (e.g., subsidized input, credit, and infrastructural development).

The general argument about inadequate incentives and resources for agriculture and rural development is valid for practically all African countries. There are few countries that devote more than a fifth of their development budget or total investment to rural areas. The lack of agricultural research, scarcity of credit schemes for peasants and pastoralists, inadequate and irregular supply of agricultural inputs, poor extension services, costly and unreliable transport and marketing facilities, and scarcity of basic consumer goods—all these have been abundantly documented in a large number of African countries.[12] There is reason to believe that in many countries the situation in this respect has deteriorated considerably in recent years.

These factors have probably had a stronger negative effect on agricultural performance than the price levels that have received far more attention in the literature. Our study in fact shows that at least in the 1970s the trend in real producer prices for food crops was favorable in the great majority of African countries, while the trend for cash crop prices was mixed with more falls than rises—in several cases due to the changes in world prices. In any case, there is much greater country diversity with respect to trends in agricultural prices than is generally recognized. Our data do not show any correlation between producer prices and overall agricultural performance. This does not, of course, mean that producer prices have no effect on production of individual crops, but that total agricultural output is influenced by a wide variety of factors.

• SUMMARY •

In this chapter we have reviewed several hypotheses that have been put forward to explain the agricultural crisis in sub-Saharan Africa. Although for analytical convenience these have been discussed separately, it is clear that several of them are overlapping and interdependent, forming part of an integrated process. They highlight factors that have contributed in varying degrees to the emergence and intensification of the crisis in one or another country or group of countries. It is perhaps inevitable that in reviewing the experience of over 30 countries it should be difficult to assess the relative importance of different factors.

Our own view is that while there have been some exogenous and short-term influences that have intensified the crisis in individual countries over specific periods, over a longer period there are two tendencies that may have been especially important. The first concerns the transition from shifting to settled agriculture and the second the inadequacy of resources and incentives for the rural sector. The problems associated with the first have been compounded by population pressure, environmental deterioration, and lack of appropriate technological innovations. It should be stressed that this is a uniquely African situation. Irrespective of the socioeconomic system and development strategies, these problems would need to be confronted and appropriate solutions found for sustained growth of agricultural production. As concerns the issue of resources and incentives for the rural sector, it is likely that the question of relative prices has been overemphasized at the expense of such aspects as adequate transport and marketing facilities, credit, research and extension services, and availability of consumer goods.

• NOTES •

1. Echoes of this hypothesis can be found in such diverse publications as World Bank, *Accelerated Development in Sub-Saharan Africa: An Agenda for Action* (The Berg Report) (Washington, D.C., 1981); Organization of African Unity, *Lagos Plan of Action for the Economic Development of Africa, 1980–2000* (Addis Ababa: OAU, 1980); R. Palmer and N. Parsons, eds., *Roots of Rural Poverty in Central and Southern Africa* (London: Heinemann, 1977); and Mohamed Lamine Gakou, *Crise de l'agriculture africaine* (Paris: Editions Silex, 1984).

2. See, among others, Palmer and Parsons, *Roots of Rural Poverty;* E. A. Brett, *Colonialism and Underdevelopment in East Africa: The Politics of Economic Change, 1919–1939* (London: Heinemann, 1973).

3. OAU, *Lagos Plan of Action;* and World Bank, *Accelerated Development.*

4. Mohamed Lamine Gakou, *Crise de l'agriculture africaine;* and Samir Amin et al., *L'agriculture et le capitalisme en Afrique* (Paris: Editions Anthropos, 1975).

5. Iftikhar Ahmed and Bill H. Kinsey, eds., *Farm Equipment Innovations in Eastern and Central Southern Africa* (Aldershot: Gower, 1984); and J. W. Mellor, C. L. Delgado, and M. J. Blackie, eds., *Accelerating Food Production and Growth in Sub-Saharan Africa* (Baltimore, Md.: Johns Hopkins University Press, forthcoming).

6. Mellor et al., *Accelerating Food Production.*

7. *Africa in Crisis: The Causes, the Cures of Environmental Bankruptcy* (London: Earthscan, 1985); Peter J. Mathon and Dustan S. Spencer, "Increasing Food Production in Sub-Saharan Africa: Environmental Problems and Inadequate Technological Solutions," *American Journal of Agricultural Economics* (December 1984).

8. See World Bank, *Accelerated Development;* and *Toward Sustained Development in Sub-Saharan Africa* (Washington, D.C., 1984); Mesfin Wolde Mariam, *Rural Vulnerability to Famine in Ethiopia: 1958–1977* (New Delhi: Vikas, 1984); Keith Hart, *The Political Economy of West African Agriculture* (Cambridge: Cambridge University Press, 1982).

9. Various World Bank publications and C. K. Eicher, "Facing Up to Africa's Food Crisis," *Foreign Affairs* (1982). Hamid Tabatabai, "Food Crisis and Development Policies in Sub-Saharan Africa," Working paper, ILO, 1985.

10. M. Lipton, *The Way People Stay Poor: A Study of Urban Bias in World Development* (London: Temple Smith, 1977); R. K. Bates, *Markets and States in Tropical Africa* (Berkeley: University of California Press, 1981).

11. Bates, *Markets and States;* K. Cleaver, *The Impact of Price and Exchange Rate Policies on Agriculture in Sub-Saharan Africa,* World Bank Staff Working Paper, 1984.

12. Judith Heyer, Pepe Roberts, and Gavin Williams, eds., *Rural Development in Tropical Africa* (New York: St. Martin's Press, 1981).

·PART 2·
Agricultural Prices, Marketing Structures, and Equity Impact

·5·

Pricing Policy and Practice

One of the central themes of the Berg Report is that inadequate incentives are a prime reason for the current poor agricultural performance in the region, and price adjustments are a major way of providing these incentives. The purpose of this chapter is to examine the ways in which price policy can be used to achieve a variety of government objectives and the difficulties of actually achieving these objectives through pricing instruments, given the conditions commonly found in sub-Saharan Africa.

· THE IMPORTANCE OF PRICES ·

The theoretical role of prices in a fully integrated market economy is well known and can be briefly summarized. First, prices determine the barter terms of trade on which goods, services, and resources can be exchanged for each other. Secondly, prices of final goods, services, and resources, along with the technical properties of the production function, determine the profitability of any production process. Thirdly, the price and volume of commodities or resources sold by individuals determine their money income, while the value of resources or commodities they own determines their wealth.

Any change in the price of a commodity or resource thus has the ability to affect the relative substitutability of goods and the demand for them, the profitability of any production process and hence the resources devoted to it, and the money incomes and wealth of resource owners. The latter affects their ability to demand goods and services and to invest in existing or new production possibilities. Very often changes in the relative price of a good or resource may have a marked impact on the demand or supply of that particular item (depending on the size of the change) and a limited effect on other related goods or resources, but very little obvious effect on the prices of the vast majority of items.

Because of the importance of the agricultural and food sectors in the economies of the region, manipulation of agricultural and food prices is one of the major policy instruments available to a government for stimulating output, reallocating resources, or altering and shifting purchasing power within the economy. Many different objectives can be influenced by agricultural policy, and although governments rarely make explicit statements about their policy goals some of the most common include:

1. Encouraging food production in order to achieve self-sufficiency, especially in staple foods

2. Stimulating export commodity production to generate additional foreign exchange earnings

3. Increasing the flow of raw materials to domestic manufacturing and processing industries

4. Stabilizing prices to agricultural producers

5. Raising rural incomes

6. Stabilizing food prices to urban consumers and restricting food price rises in an attempt to reduce inflationary pressures on the economy

7. Generating government revenues by taxing the surpluses of the agricultural sector in various ways

8. Assisting domestic industries by making agricultural raw materials available to them at prices below those that would otherwise exist

9. Encouraging specific forms of production, organization, and social and economic transformation such as cooperatives, collectives, state farms, private sector plantations, smallholdings, etc.

• THE CONSEQUENCES OF MANIPULATING PRICES: THE ECONOMIC AND POLITICAL TRADE-OFFS •

It is fairly obvious that several of these goals are conflicting, and yet governments may still pursue them or at least pay lip-service to them in an attempt to appease different pressure groups within society. If a government relies primarily on pricing as its major instrument for implementing policies, conflicts between achieving different objectives will inevitably result. Even where an apparently non-conflicting set of objectives is chosen, attempting to achieve them all through a single pricing instrument may create conflicts and inconsistencies.

With food as a major component in the expenditure pattern of low income urban dwellers, any marked increase in the price of food to encourage food production or raise rural incomes can have a significant effect on the urban workers' standard of living, leading to demands for higher wages and creating inflationary pressures in the economy. Moreover, attempts to increase food prices suddenly, as in the Sudan in early 1985, have frequently been the overt reason for strikes, riots, and on some occasions revolutions. However, attempts to hold down consumer price increases through subsidies can put a considerable strain on government budgets, leading to increased borrowing from the central bank and an expansion in the money supply that in itself can be inflationary. The United Republic of Tanzania, Zambia, and Zimbabwe all experienced problems arising from escalating consumer subsidies in the 1970s. Some alternatives are an increase in taxation, which in some countries means increasing the duty on agricultural exports; allowing the exchange rate to become overvalued, thus reducing the domestic price of food imports; or suppressing the price paid to agricultural producers of food crops. Examples of these various techniques are given in Chapter 7. All of these can have profound effects on the functioning of the economy, the level of food production, and income distribution within the economy.

There is also a potential conflict between achieving domestic objectives through the price mechanism and maintaining an external balance. There has been a tendency to consider agricultural and food pricing issues in a partial equilibrium, closed–economy framework. However, the importance of the agricultural sector for foreign exchange earnings, the high import content of the agricultural inputs required for "modern" farming techniques, the increasing importance of food imports, and the long land boundaries between contiguous countries in the sub-Saharan region mean that agricultural and food pricing has to be conducted in an open–economy framework in order to be effective. The choice of an appropriate foreign exchange rate can have a considerable effect on both the performance and fortunes of the agricultural sector, the overall balance of payments, and the growth of the economy. Many African countries appear to be paying a high price now for neglecting this consideration.

• THE ABILITY TO INFLUENCE PRICES IN PRACTICE •

Difficulties of Decision-making

Given the importance of the agricultural and food sectors in the economy, it is not surprising to find that governments of all political complexions attempt to intervene in the agricultural and food pricing process. The methods they use will be examined shortly, but first we wish to examine some of the doubts raised concerning the effectiveness of the pricing mechanism, particularly in the rural sector of many sub-Saharan African countries.

The doubts arise in part because the price mechanism works most effectively when all resources and commodities are traded in markets that are well integrated and competitive. Even in these circumstances, with commercially-oriented, profit-maximizing farmers, the actual production decisions will be influenced not only by absolute price changes but by the relative changes in the prices of different commodities and resources. Furthermore, because of the length of many agricultural production processes, particularly for tree crops, there is frequently a lagged response to any price change. Thus we would not necessarily find a simple positive correlation between an increased price for a particular commodity and its output.

When we consider agricultural production in sub-Saharan Africa, the situation is even more complex. In large parts of the region a substantial proportion of goods and resources is not traded and many of the markets that do exist are extremely fragmented. There are several reasons that account for this situation. First, the lack of an effective transport system means that some areas are geographically isolated from the major marketing channels for certain commodities and resources. In these areas in particular, the degree of monetization may be very low and price movements may have a very limited effect on resource allocation.

Secondly, throughout the region there is still a marked tendency for farm households to attempt to be self-sufficient for a large proportion of their basic food requirements even when cash crops can be produced and sold. It may be that a certain degree of satisfaction is derived from self-sufficiency, but more probably this reflects a defensive reaction against the failure of the marketing system to provide a continuous and reliable supply of food at a reasonable price. In these circumstances there is considerable doubt concerning the effect of movements in the price of food crops on the production and marketing of food. Many farmers will sell a part of their food crops when they have a surplus to their own requirements or when they need to generate cash for other purposes. This type of farmer may not react, or may react extremely slowly, to changes in the price of food crops, particularly if he thinks these changes are only temporary.

Thirdly, in some areas some types of resources may not be traded. This tends to reduce resource mobility and the effectiveness of the price mechanism. One example of this is the absence of a land market due to a social tradition of land being held under communal tenure or due to legislation preventing the sale of land. Again, in some circumstances there may be very little labor hiring, perhaps due to social custom or the low degree of monetization in the economy.

Fourthly, due to the ineffective functioning of markets some of the resources required to expand production, such as high yielding seeds and fertilizers, may be unobtainable in some localities. In such cases, raising the price of the end product per se is unlikely to elicit much of an overall production response, although the limited resources available may be shifted from other uses in these circumstances. A similar consideration may apply to the aggregate output response to price increases where there is a labor shortage at peak times.

Taking all four of these factors into account, we find that in many circumstances there is not a clear and unequivocal response of output to a change in the price of a product. Deficiencies and errors in the available data regarding prices and production further confound this situation, and this is why we have not pursued an empirical investigation of the links between prices and production in Chapter 6.

There are also deficiencies at the policy-making level that weaken the effectiveness of the pricing mechanism. A major reason is the lack of skilled manpower and information needed for effective price formulation in this complex environment. Many countries in the region do not have sufficient professionals to allocate to this task or do not appreciate the benefits to be derived from devoting more attention to an appropriate set of prices. The limited number of people working in this area are hampered by the lack of sound data on which to base their analyses.

The problem of inadequate analysis is reinforced when pricing decisions affecting different commodities or resources are made in a variety of government departments or quasi-governmental marketing organizations. For instance, it is not uncommon to find the prices for some agricultural products being set by the Ministry of Agriculture and for others by the separate, semi-autonomous marketing organizations. At the same time, a Ministry of Commerce may be responsible for fixing agricultural input prices, such as fertilizer prices, the marketing margins on domestically consumed agricultural products, and even the retail price of a range of food items. However, the "price" of other inputs, such as the interest rate for government sponsored agricultural credit schemes and the foreign exchange rate that affects the domestic price of agricultural exports and imported agricultural inputs, may be set by a Ministry of Finance. Very often, the interdepartmental machinery necessary for coordination of these various pricing decisions is inadequate or completely nonexistent. Very few countries have fully fledged interministerial committees to analyze and coordinate pricing decisions.[1] Sometimes two ministries will jointly agree on a pricing decision—for example, to raise both the producer and the consumer price of a food item—and then one ministry may delay the implementation of the part for which it is responsible. For instance, a minimum producer price may be raised by the Ministry of Agriculture, but a complementary decision to raise the consumer price may be delayed by the Ministry of Commerce, creating considerable problems for the marketing agencies that have to operate on reduced margins in the meantime.

The development of a consistent pricing policy is further aggravated when major policy decisions are announced by leading politicians or officials without prior or adequate discussions with the rest of the government or civil service.[2] Frequently such pronouncements are made to alleviate acute political problems emanating from particular groups or to make immediate political gains, but the long run repercussions are very often much worse than the true magnitude of the original problem.

The Problems of Implementation

In practice there is a huge gap between announcing a desired price and establishing it as the actual price. Many governments lack the administrative machinery, controls and infrastructure to implement the pricing decisions effectively once they are made. Governments that wish to intervene in agricultural and food pricing face two broad options. They must either implement the policy through private traders, or they must enter the marketing system themselves.

Price Implementation Through Private Traders

Taking the first approach, the government may attempt to impose mandatory pricing rules on traders. However, this requires effective policing and involves at least three problems. First, there is often insufficient manpower to ensure that the announced prices are being implemented. Secondly, in the absence of rigorous control there is a tendency for the inspectors themselves to engage in bribery and corruption, thus negating the effects of the price controls.[3] Thirdly, for many commodities there is a variety of market outlets for producers to choose among, particularly for those living close to border areas where goods can be smuggled to neighboring countries. This enormously increases the problems of policing the price controls. The large numbers of producers, consumers, and market outlets; the small size of many transactions; the absence of records; the high costs in manpower, transport, etc. of operating a policing service all tend to reinforce the inevitable conclusion that in the vast majority of sub-Saharan African countries the implementation of government pricing policies through legislation and policing alone is most unlikely to succeed.

In these circumstances one option is for the government to limit its pricing and policing activities to areas it considers most critical, or where it considers it has the greatest chance of success. A key criterion for effective control is a limited range of outlets for a commodity at some stage in the marketing process. Four main commodity groups become obvious candidates for pricing intervention using this criterion, but the end result is the introduction of some peculiar biases into the pricing system.

The first major commodity group includes products that are shipped overseas and must therefore pass through a limited number of port outlets. If a government's sole intention is to impose an export tax, then it can achieve this without actively engaging in marketing itself, although this may not work where supplies can be smuggled through land boundaries to countries operating more favorable pricing regimes. Cocoa smuggling between West African states is the classic example of this. If the intention is to influence producer prices for export crops, one method is to use a licensed buyer system, perhaps granting each buyer sole purchasing rights for the commodity in a particular geographical area. This reduces the task of policing the pricing system to more manageable proportions, but failure to implement effective policing can lead to considerable abuse of the monopsony powers, particularly where producers also rely on the traders for supplies of agricultural inputs or credit. Fixed prices, minimum prices, seasonal prices, and quality differentials can all be implemented through this system providing the trader is given sufficient financial incentive to collect the produce and transport it to its destination. This proviso is particularly important where pan-territorial producer pricing is practiced where otherwise there may be no incentive to market produce from remote areas.

The second major commodity group in which intervention is relatively easy, and in which governments may wish to intervene actively to influence either producer or consumer prices, includes those foodstuffs that at some stage (preferably near the point of consumption) pass through a restricted number of marketing channels. An almost universal example nowadays is grain milling in larger urban areas, which is carried out in relatively large–scale industrial plants. This makes the grain mills a useful focal point for establishing a price regime that can be extended forward into the retail stages for grain–derived products such as maize and wheat flour, bread, etc., and perhaps backward to producers. Control over the price of these products is of particular importance to governments because of their significance in the consumption expenditure of the mass of the urban population. The importance of a restriction in the marketing channel to implement effective price control is well illustrated by grain products because price control is rarely as effective for whole grains or those processed in small plants, where policing is more difficult and costly. Thus effective price controls often exist for the "superior" cereal products but not for millet and sorghum, which are rarely processed in large–scale plants. For this reason it is even easier to control the price of imported grain products since virtually complete control can be obtained over the marketing channels. Again, price controls are often more effective for refined sugar and vegetable oils than for less refined qualities produced in small–scale plants. Several other food items more frequently consumed by middle- to high-income households—e.g., pasteurized milk and high quality meat—are often processed in large–scale plants, and it is not unusual to find effective price controls for these products, partly because of the ease of intervention and partly as a favor to these politically powerful groups.

At the other extreme, virtually no country attempts to control the price of fruit and vegetables because of the multitude of marketing channels and outlets, their seasonality, perishability, and wide range of qualities. Thus, in most countries price intervention for foodstuffs centers mainly on those processed grain products consumed by the mass of the urban population. For these products effective price controls may also be reflected back to the producer prices of supplies sold in "official" marketing channels but may be less effective for local sales. For most other food products in whose case control over marketing channels is more difficult, price intervention is likely to be much less effective, at both the retail and the producer levels.

The third commodity group that lends itself to price intervention includes those non-food crops that may be used domestically but require processing between the producer and final consumer stages. For instance, seed cotton requires ginning to produce cotton lint. Other industrial crops that are normally exported but require domestic processing, such as sisal, pyrethrum, etc., are also potential candidates for price control but face the problem that world prices may fluctuate. The introduction of fixed domestic prices may cause severe financing problems for the exporting agencies unless some price stabilization system is available.

The other major area where price intervention may be relatively easy is for manufactured, centrally produced, or imported agricultural inputs such as fertilizer,[4] chemicals, hybrid seeds, and machinery, and also in the provision of formal sector agricultural finance. In all these cases supplies emanate from a very limited number of sources and sometimes there are only single market channels available. In these circumstances it is quite feasible to impose fixed pricing and even pan-territorial uniform pricing of inputs as cross-subsidization of variable transport costs can be internalized. Subsidization of inputs and credit, subject to the limits of government finance, can also be introduced fairly readily. Whether these various practices are desirable on grounds of either efficiency or equity is highly debatable. There is a tendency for higher–income farmers to use or to obtain easier access to purchased agricultural inputs and credit, and to the extent that these are subsidized there are obvious income distribution implications.

Government Participation in Marketing

Alternatives to relying on private traders to implement pricing policy are the encouragement of government-controlled producer cooperatives or the creation of some form of government marketing organization. Governments may, of course, decide to become actively engaged in the physical marketing of commodities for a variety of reasons, and in many countries government agencies are responsible for the marketing of export crops, the marketing and milling of major grain products, and the distribution of fertilizer and agricultural credit. While this may eliminate much of the potential for exploitation implicit in the licensed trader system, experience has shown that cooperatives and government organizations do not always serve their members effectively or equally, sometimes concentrating their attention on certain groups of farmers and particular geographical areas and using their own monopsony positions to exploit producers in much the same ways as private traders. Thus there is not necessarily any reduction in the need for effective policing. Moreover, as we have already seen in Chapter 4, control over the agricultural marketing system also brings with it control over substantial resource flows, which governments may use for their own purposes or allow different groups or individuals to enjoy as a way of dispensing political patronage. Examples of the extent of this practice are given in Chapters 7 and 8.

As a result, there can be confusion of objectives and the pricing instrument may be used in very different ways from those originally intended. Even in the absence of this complicating factor, governments may set the marketing organizations' objectives and then not provide the facilities or finance necessary to fulfill them. For instance, the government may set a relatively high producer price and a relatively low consumer price, the margin between being too small for the marketing organization to finance the purchase, storage, and distribution of sufficient supplies to satisfy urban consumers' requirements without borrowing funds.[5] In these circumstances the marketing organization will frequently concentrate its attention on that part of the total supply that it can market most cheaply. There are several instances, particularly in west Africa,[6] in which this has meant that the government marketing organizations have preferred to handle imported supplies rather than the domestic crop, particularly when the latter involves high transport costs. Similar considerations apply to the preference of many governments for pan-territorial pricing for outputs and inputs. Unless the transport costs are met by the government or can be financed from within the organization, there will be a tendency to concentrate the marketing facilities on the areas that involved least transport costs.

At other times, the government may set prices that are so out of line with those that would obtain in a free market that conditions of either considerable excess demand or excess supply are created. For instance, the government may set a very low consumer price and consequently a low producer price, allowing the marketing organization a "reasonable" margin to perform its functions. But this low price may generate a large demand, particularly if the price of substitute goods is not fixed in this manner. At the same time, producers may be unwilling either to produce the good at the low price they are offered or to sell their supplies to the marketing organization at these prices. This is illustrated by the development of parallel markets in many instances, and the ineffectiveness of food marketing boards in several countries.[7]

A frequent complaint of farmers is the delay by government agencies in paying when crop deliveries have been made. Furthermore, government agencies frequently fail to provide the same range of facilities as private traders, especially credit facilities, and farmers thus prefer to deal with private traders. In these circumstances, both the prices and the government marketing organization tend to become inoperative. Consumers are willing to pay higher prices than the official price to obtain supplies of the commodity, private traders are willing to offer producers higher prices to obtain the supplies, and vigorous parallel markets are created even though they may be illegal. Governments may attempt to coerce farmers to sell their supplies to them but there are many ways in which peasant farmers in particular can avoid this coercion.

• CONCLUSION •

The gap between the role of price policy in theory and its effective application in most sub-Saharan African countries is very wide. In practice we find that the prices governments desire to implement very often apply to only a limited percentage of the total quantity of the commodity being produced and traded. Very often two-tier pricing systems are in operation with wide divergences between the official and unofficial market prices and this has considerable effects on both efficiency and equity. Some consumers may be fortunate to purchase foodstuffs at official or subsidized prices, but the large mass of consumers have to pay a much higher price. Some producers are able to buy inputs or obtain credit at low prices; many others are deprived because the government cannot finance any more subsidized supplies. Some producers may be forced to sell their produce to marketing organizations at low prices while others may be able to sell at higher prices elsewhere. But equally, in years of glut some producers may be fortunate enough to sell their produce to the marketing organizations at the official price while others may have to accept a much lower price.

Even the entry of the government into the marketing process is not sufficient to guarantee the implementation of their desired pricing policy. To achieve this they must have substantial control over the marketing system. Paradoxically, for products with multiple outlets, such as food, this can often be obtained only by setting prices somewhere near those that would obtain in a free market situation. Even when the marketing system is under effective control producers can often switch their resources to other commodities if they are dissatisfied with those offered by the government.

Our argument is that because of their lack of effective control over markets, governments in the region have much less influence over agricultural and food prices than is sometimes imagined. Only when producers have limited options or are producing commodities at very low opportunity cost are governments able to distort producer prices markedly below equilibrium or world market price levels. This will occur more frequently for export crops than domestic food crops, and we attempt to justify this statement by an empirical examination of agricultural price trends in the next chapter.

• NOTES •

1. For a review see FAO, *Agricultural Price Policies in Africa: Lessons and Experience,* Thirteenth Regional Conference for Africa, Harare, Zimbabwe, 16–25 July 1984 (Rome: FAO, ARC/84/4 May 1984), pp. 33.

2. Such as the sudden announcement by President Jomo Kenyatta of a dramatic rise in the producer price of milk at an agricultural show in 1971. The consequent upsurge in marketed milk (aided by favorable rains) to the Kenya Co-operative Creameries ultimately caused a financial crisis for this organization.

3. In Kenya, movement controls for maize used to reinforce price controls led to widespread bribery and corruption. See G. Schmidt, "Maize and Beans in Kenya: The Interaction and Effectiveness of Formal and Informal Marketing Systems," Institute for Development Studies, Occasional Paper No. 31 (Nairobi University, 1979), p. 31.

4. Virtually every government in sub-Saharan Africa intervenes in fertilizer pricing. See FAO, *Agricultural Price Policies.*

5. This was one of the problems encountered by the National Milling Cooperation of the United Republic of Tanzania. See Sigma One Corporation, *The Consumption Effects of Agricultural Policies in Tanzania* (Washington, D.C.: USAID, January 1982).

6. H. Creupelandt, "Food Marketing Boards in the Sahel and West Africa" (Mimeographed paper presented at a seminar on Marketing Boards in Tropical Africa, Leiden, Holland, 19–23 September 1983), pp. 13.

7. Ibid.

·6·

Price Performance in the 1970s

One of the generalizations made about the patterns of agricultural pricing in sub-Saharan Africa over the past decade is that there have been inadequate price incentives for agricultural producers. In particular it is alleged that export crops have been heavily taxed and that food crop prices have been deliberately set below equilibrium levels in an attempt to reduce consumer price levels.[1] In this chapter we analyze the official price data for the major food and export crops in the 1970s for as many sub-Saharan countries as possible. We have reservations concerning the quality of the data available (see Appendix 1). Furthermore, our choice of methodology, discussed in Appendix 1, was influenced by the types of information available. Despite these limitations, our examination suggests that some of the sweeping generalizations made about agricultural and food prices in the region may be misplaced, particularly concerning food crop prices. On the other hand, the evidence suggests that in some countries export crops were heavily taxed in the 1970s. We examine the implications of these for agricultural incomes and equity in Chapter 8. We examine first empirical evidence on the real consumer price of food, the real producer price of food crops, and the relationship between domestic and international food crop prices. We then analyze the real producer price of cash crops and compare domestic and international cash crop prices.

· THE EMPIRICAL EVIDENCE ·

The Consumer Price of Food

If governments have attempted to restrict the increase in consumer food prices, they have not been entirely successful. As shown in Chapter 2 (Table 2.7), over the past decade there has been a tendency for consumer food prices to rise in almost all African countries for which data are available.

68

Only in Zimbabwe was there a statistically significant fall in the consumer price of food relative to the general cost of living. In Ghana, the United Republic of Tanzania, and the Côte–d'Ivoire the rise was particularly rapid, and there were undoubtedly other countries without complete price series where the rise was as severe.

Given the importance of food in the overall cost of living index in most countries, the inference is that the consumer price of food was rising much faster than the price of non-food items in the 1970s. In some situations the food price rise could have been even faster than the official figures suggest because in certain countries the food shortages led to the development of parallel markets, with food being sold at prices far in excess of the official ones. Further evidence from a limited number of retail price series for individual foods is discussed in the case studies presented in the next chapter.

The Real Producer Price of Food Products

If the consumer price of food has risen in this fashion, we might expect producer prices to have risen as well, unless the cost of marketing or the surpluses extracted by marketing agencies have risen very rapidly. To examine this issue, as part of the first exercise (see Appendix 1) the trends in real producer prices were calculated for the three food crops contributing most calories to the domestically produced food supply. Complete series for 1969 to 1980 were available for only eleven countries, but another five had series spanning at least ten years, i.e., 1969 to 1979 or 1970 to 1980. Some caution has to be exercised in comparing results from countries where different time periods are used (Table 6.1). This table indicates a wide variety of pricing patterns and also the considerable variation in food production and consumption patterns between countries, but on balance there were more statistically significant producer price increases than decreases for the commodities surveyed. This tendency is reinforced if the signs of the nonsignificant coefficients are also examined. In only two countries, Nigeria and Somalia, were the signs of all surveyed food crop price coefficients negative; but in five countries, Burkina Faso, Ghana, Niger, Kenya, and Swaziland, all signs were positive. It is known that in Nigeria, at least, the prices refer to official purchasing prices, and the actual market prices are likely to have exceeded these.

This general picture of a majority of upward movements in real prices is supported by an analysis of trends in the real price of three food crops— maize, rice (paddy), and groundnuts—for all countries with price and production data over the period 1968–1980 (Table 6.2) conducted as part of the second exercise. For each of the three commodities there were more price increases than decreases. The implicit rate of growth of real gross income

Table 6.1 Average Annual Rate of Growth in the Real Producer Price of Major Food Products in Sixteen Sub-Saharan Countries (Percentage Per Year)

Country and Time Period	Commodities	Domestic Supply as Percentage of Average Daily Calorie Intake (1975–77)	Annual Rate of Growth in Real Price Percentage Per Year	Country and Time Period	Commodities	Domestic Supply as Percentage of Average Daily Calorie Intake (1975–77)	Annual Rate of Growth in Real Price Percentage Per Year
Cameroon (1969–80)	Maize	18	3.4	Burkina Faso (1969–80)	Sorghum	41	2.8
	Millet	15	–1.7		Millet	24	2.2
	Groundnuts	10	3.7		Dry cowpeas	6	1.3
Central African Republic (1969–80)	Cassava	39	–4.2	Zaire (1969–80)	Cassava	56	16.5
	Groundnuts	12	–0.9 ns		Maize	7	9.5
	Yams	9	0.2		Palm oil	5	–2.0
Ghana (1969–80)	Cassava	19	1.9 ns	Zambia (1969–80)	Maize	53	1.2
	Maize	12	5.1		Sugar	8	–3.7
	Toro Cocovam	11	0.9 ns		Cassava	5	7.9
Madagascar (1969–80)	Rice	53	3.1	Zimbabwe (1979–80)	Maize	55	–0.5 ns
	Cassava	10	na		Millet	11	na
	Maize	5	–0.8 ns		Sugar	8	–0.7 ns
Nigeria (1969–80)	Sorghum	17	–4.0	Kenya (1969–79)	Maize	44	2.1
	Yams	16	–7.9		Pulses N.E.S.	7	1.6 ns
	Millet	13	–5.5		Sugar	6	2.3
Niger (1969–80)	Millet	47	2.6	Malawi (1969–79)	Maize	65	–1.4
	Sorghum	16	4.1		Groundnuts	6	1.8
	Dry cowpeas	12	0.9 ns				

Sierra Leone (1969–80)	Rice	50	−0.2 ns	Somalia (1969–79)	Sorghum	16	−5.5
	Palm oil	17	2.2 ns		Maize	13	−5.5
					Sugar	5	na
United Republic of Tanzania (1969–80)	Cassava	24	−2.1	Swaziland (1969–79)	Maize	30	0.9 ns
	Maize	21	3.3		Sugar cane	19	6.5

Analysis of the Annual Rate of Growth in Real Price

	Negative	Positive	Positive ns	Negative ns	na
1st product	5	7	2	2	0
2nd product	4	7	2	1	2
3rd product	2	3	4	2	5
TOTAL	11	17	8	5	7

ns: not statistically significant at the 0.1 level
na: not available

Table 6.2 Trends in Food Crop Pricing and Production, 1968–80

Countries Ranked by Production Level 1978–80 Average Per Year	Net Exports '000 nt 1968–70	Net Exports '000 nt 1978–80	Compound Annual Percentage Rate of Growth of: Real Producer Price 1968–80	World Representative Price[a] in Real Domestic Terms 1968–80	Simple Average Ratio of Producer Price at Official Exchange Rate to World Representative Price 1968–70	Simple Average Ratio of Producer Price at Official Exchange Rate to World Representative Price 1978–80	Compound Annual Percentage Rate of Growth of: Production (quantity) 1968–80	Real Gross Income 1968–80
Maize								
> 1 million tons								
Kenya	154	–60	1.3	–0.2ns	0.62	0.72	–0.5ns	0.8
United Republic of Tanzania	11	–66	2.6	–0.9ns	0.55	0.74	8.2	10.8
Nigeria	–3	–108	–4.6	–6.5	1.24	1.67	3.4	–1.2
Zimbabwe	259	218	–0.4	2.2	0.79	0.61	1.7ns	1.3
Malawi	14	–4	–1.5	1.5ns	0.56	0.43	1.1	–0.4
Zambia	5	–124	1.0	0.9ns	0.89	0.98	4.3	5.3
100,000 to 1 million tons								
Zaire	–55	–144	8.2	–7.8	0.50	2.94	2.5	10.7
Cameroon	—	—	3.3	–2.2	0.92	1.67	2.1	5.4
Ghana	–2	–53	5.4	–12.1	1.04	4.67	–2.1	5.4
Côte-d'Ivoire	–4	–13	–2.5	–3.2	0.71	0.78	1.5	–1.0
Madagascar	2	2	0.8ns	–0.2ns	0.58	0.76	–0.3ns	0.5
Somalia	1	–32	–6.1	–2.3	1.25	0.81	0.2ns	–5.9
Burkina Faso	—	–3	1.2	0.0ns	0.95	1.23	1.2ns	2.4
<100,000 tons								
Senegal	–20	–14	1.7	–2.0	0.73	1.10	5.0	6.7
Central African Republic	—	—	0.5ns	–1.5ns	0.81	1.07	–2.3	–1.8
Sierra Leone	—	–1	–0.5ns	2.3	0.62	0.47	2.2	1.7

Rice Paddy							
>500,000 tons							
Madagascar	56	−130	3.6	−1.8ns	0.43	0.73	0.9	4.5
Nigeria	−1	−510	−6.5	−7.9	1.57	1.93	7.1	0.6
Sierra Leone	−30	−58	−0.4ns	−0.7	0.97	0.86	2.0	1.6
Côte-d'Ivoire	−61	−192	2.6ns	−4.7	0.70	1.38	4.8	7.4
100,000 to 500,000 tons							
United Republic of Tanzania	−10	−58	−1.1	−2.5	0.68	0.75	3.3	2.2
Senegal	−150	−289	−2.5	−3.5	0.72	0.79	0.8ns	−1.7
<100,000 tons							
Ghana	−37	−37	14.3	−13.5	0.75	7.37	4.0	18.3
Cameroon	−9	−25	10.5	−3.7	0.44	1.87	15.7	26.2
Kenya	−1	−4	2.1	−1.8ns	0.60	0.96	5.5	7.6
Malawi	1	7	−2.2	−0.1ns	0.62	0.50	9.7	7.5
Niger	—	−25	−0.1ns	−4.1	0.63	0.95	−2.8	−2.9
Central African Republic	—	—	4.8	−3.0	0.60	1.27	4.9	9.7

Table 6.2 Continued

Countries Ranked by Production Level 1978–80 Average Per Year	Net Exports as a Percentage of Gross Production 1975–77	Compound Annual Percentage Rate of Growth of: Real Producer Price 1968–80	World Representative Price[a] in Real Domestic Terms 1968–80	Simple Average Ratio of Producer Price at Official Exchange Rate to World Representative Price 1968–70	1978–80	Compound Annual Percentage Rate of Growth of: Production (quantity) 1968–80	Real Gross Income 1968–80
Groundnuts in Shell							
>500,000 tons							
Senegal	72	-0.1	-1.2 ns	0.49	0.55	-0.6 ns	-0.7
Nigeria	-8	8.6	-5.7	0.40	1.61	-12.6	-4.0
100,000 to 500,000 tons							
Zaire	0	14.8	-7.1	0.29	2.14	2.7	17.5
Malawi	22	1.8	2.3	0.58	0.62	-0.8 ns	1.0
Cameroon	4	3.5	-1.4 ns	0.82	1.39	-2.9	0.6
Central African Republic	0	-1.0 ns	-0.7 ns	0.73	0.68	6.1	5.1
Zimbabwe	0	5.9	3.0	0.74	0.96	-0.1 ns	5.8
<100,000 tons							
Ghana	0	6.9	-11.4	0.94	5.64	2.5	9.4
Niger	24	4.3	-1.8 ns	0.35	0.60	-10.0	-5.7
Burkina Faso	14	-1.9	0.8 ns	0.44	0.39	0.0 ns	-1.9
Côte-d'Ivoire	-7	-7.9	-2.4	0.63	0.34	3.2	-4.7
United Republic of Tanzania	-7	3.7	-0.1 ns	1.02	1.41	3.8	7.5
Madagascar	2	0.6 ns	0.6 ns	0.63	0.63	-0.3 ns	0.3
Zambia	-7	6.1	1.7 ns	0.97	1.46	-8.1	-2.0
Sierra Leone	-3	0.6 ns	3.2	0.67	0.56	-4.1	-3.5
Kenya	0	-1.4	0.6 ns	0.76	0.59	11.2	9.8
Somalia	0	-8.5	-1.5 ns	1.23	0.58	-2.1	-10.6

Analysis of the Annual Rates of Growth in Real Price

	Negative	Positive	Positive ns	Negative ns
Maize	5	8	2	1
Rice	4	5	1	2
Groundnuts	4	9	2	2
Total	13	22	5	5

Analysis of the Annual Rates of Growth in Real Gross Income

	Negative	Positive
Maize	5	11
Rice	2	10
Groundnuts	8	9
Total	15	30

na: not statistically significant at the 0.1 level
ns: not available
a For maize, Argentine maize c.i.f. North Sea ports.
For rice, Thai 5 percent broken, milled, f.o.b. Bangkok. Producer price adjusted to milled rice equivalent by variable coefficient supplied by FAO.
For groundnuts, Nigerian shelled, c.i.f. European ports. Producer price adjusted to shelled equivalent by variable coefficient provided by FAO.

also shows the number of positive coefficients exceeding the number of negative growth rates particularly for maize and rice (Table 6.2, column 7). It should be noted that as total production and not marketed production is being used, this shows not the rate of growth of real cash income but the estimated value of total production at real market (or official) prices.

Producer Prices for Food Crops and World Prices

The evidence that the majority of real food crop producer prices rose over the past decade does not resolve the question as to whether these prices were depressed below the free market equilibrium price level. The conceptual and empirical problems involved in establishing an equilibrium price and comparing the actual producer price with it are discussed in Appendix 1.

An examination of farm and world prices has been carried out for up to seventeen countries covering five commodities that are fairly widely grown and consumed and also traded internationally. For maize, rice (paddy), and groundnuts the period 1968–1980 was used, but for wheat and sugar the examination spanned the period 1966–1981.

Maize

In Table 6.2, sixteen countries are ranked in order of production in 1978–1980. The net export calculation shows that in 1968–1970 all countries except Zaire and Senegal were virtually self-sufficient in maize or, as in Kenya and Zimbabwe, had exportable surpluses. By 1978–1980 virtually all countries except Zimbabwe were net importers, with Nigeria, Zambia, and Zaire each importing, on average, more than 100,000 tons per year. Apart from Zimbabwe only Cameroon, Madagascar, and the Central African Republic were entirely self-sufficient. In these circumstances, and with other things remaining equal, we would expect the equilibrium price to rise in relation to the world price in the majority of countries because of the increasing need to import to meet the domestic deficit. When the simple average ratio of the producer price is compared to the world representative price for the periods 1968–1970 and 1978–1980, this in fact occurs for twelve of the sixteen countries being studied. The exceptions are Zimbabwe (which remained a net exporter), Malawi (which had a temporary domestic deficit), Somalia, and Sierra Leone. As Table 6.2 shows, these last two countries are relatively small producers although maize is an important food in Somalia (Table 6.1).

Of course, among other factors changes in either the producer price or the world price (or both) can affect this ratio. This can be seen clearly in

Table 6.2, where trends in the real producer price and the world representative price in real domestic terms at the official exchange rate are also shown. In some countries, such as Zimbabwe and Sierra Leone, the world price rose in real domestic terms while in most countries it fell. The lower the rate of inflation and/or the higher the rate of devaluation of the exchange rate, the greater is the tendency for the real world price to rise in domestic currency terms. On the other hand, countries with a high rate of inflation and a relatively constant exchange rate, that is, countries allowing their currencies to become overvalued (see Appendix 1), such as Ghana and Zaire, show a rapidly declining real world price.

At the same time that the real world price was declining in Ghana and Zaire, the real producer price rose rapidly due to the shortage of foreign exchange to import food and a consequent domestic food shortage. The result was that the simple average ratio of producer price to world price rose dramatically. In Nigeria, the real world price also fell markedly. The real producer price also fell but not as rapidly, leading to a moderate increase in the ratio. As discussed in Appendix 1, this result may reflect the use of an official, unrepresentative purchase price rather than an actual market price.

In Zimbabwe, Malawi, and Sierra Leone, the fall in the ratio was caused by a rise in the real world price coupled with a moderate fall in the real producer price. As these countries were in export surplus or virtually self-sufficient over that period, this slight decline in the real producer price might have been justified. However, in Somalia, where the ratio also fell, there was a sharp decline in real producer price at a time when the country was moving into import deficit. Moreover, the ratio of producer price to world price fell below 1.00. Somalia, then, emerges as the only clear example among the sixteen countries studied in which the producer price relative to the world price has moved in a different direction from what might have been anticipated in the circumstances.

Rice (Paddy)

Information on rice prices and production is available for twelve countries. Only four were not net importers in 1968–1970, and by 1978–1980 only Malawi had a small exportable surplus. Moreover, by 1978–1980 Madagascar, Nigeria, Côte–d'Ivoire, and Senegal were all importing well over 100,000 tons per year even though all were major producers by sub-Saharan African standards. As with maize, other things being equal, we would expect the ratio of producer price to world representative price to have been higher in the importing countries than in the self-sufficient countries, and perhaps to rise as the deficit continued and deepened. Both of these results broadly occur, with the ratio rising in ten of the twelve countries. The ratio fell in Malawi, which increased its exportable surplus, and also in Sierra Leone, the only country in which the real world price rose. This was in large part due to Sierra Leone's realistic exchange rate policy in the 1970s. As the fall in the producer price was statistically non-significant, and the ratio of the producer price to world price remained above 0.85, this can hardly be quoted as an example of a depressed real price.

In all other cases the real producer price either rose when the real world price fell (Ghana again providing the most extreme example) or fell less rapidly than the world price, as in Nigeria, Senegal, and the United Republic of Tanzania. In both Senegal and Tanzania these movements in real producer price were accompanied by ratios of producer price to world price of just less than 0.8 but given domestic transport costs these rates may not be below the import parity price (see Appendix 1, Table 1). Thus, for rice there is no clear evidence of producer prices being depressed below the equilibrium level.

Groundnuts

Information has been analyzed for seventeen countries, but only seven of these could be termed substantial producers. The possibility of groundnuts being processed in the country of origin and of the derived products such as groundnut oil being traded means that it is difficult to show trends in net exports as in the cases of maize and rice. However, using information from the FAO Food Balance Sheets,[2] net exports of groundnuts and groundnut products have been calculated as a percentage of gross production for the period 1975–1977. This shows that at that time Senegal, Niger, Malawi, and Burkina Faso were the only significant net exporters, with the other countries being basically self-sufficient or small net importers. Many of these latter countries had small exports of groundnuts in shell in earlier years, implying a movement to a net import position over the years.

In this situation, and with other things remaining equal, we might expect the producer price as a ratio of the world representative price to be lower in the four exporting countries than in the importing countries and might perhaps expect the ratio in the latter countries to have risen over time. These tendencies are in fact supported by the empirical evidence, the major exceptions being the Côte–d'Ivoire and Somalia. In the Côte–d'Ivoire, despite a significant importation of groundnut products, the ratio of producer price to world price has fallen from 0.63 to 0.34. The real producer price has also fallen by 7.9 percent per year. Somalia had no groundnut trade in 1975–1977, but the real producer price fell by 8.5 percent per year over the period 1968–1980, to bring the ratio of producer price to world price down from 1.23 to 0.58. These two countries together with the four exporting countries provide examples of producer prices possibly being depressed below equilibrium levels, but Nominal Protection Coefficients (NCPs, see Appendix 1) for a series of years would need to be calculated to verify this.

Wheat

Information on wheat is available for only five countries, none of which can be termed a large producer although Kenya has produced more than 0.5 million tons per year throughout the period. Although production has increased in each of the countries over the 1966–1968 to 1979–1981 period, this has not prevented the import deficit, already present in four of the countries in 1966–1968, from increasing in virtually all countries over this period (Table 6.3).

In those circumstances one might expect prices to be around the import parity level throughout the period to give some encouragement to

Table 6.3 The Relationship Between Producer Prices and World Representative Prices for Food Crops, 1966–81

Countries Ranked by Production Level 1979–81 Average Per Year	Net Exports Million Tons		Simple Average Ratio of Producer Price to Representative World Price	
	1966–68	1979–81	1966–68	1979–81
Wheat				
>100,000 Tons Per Year				
Ethiopia	−0.003	−0.245	1.31	1.20
Kenya	0.035	−0.038	1.21	1.18
< 100,000 Tons Per Year				
United Republic of Tanzania	−0.028	−0.927	1.28	1.23
Zambia	−0.041	−0.133	1.26	1.89
Cameroon	−0.015	−0.064	0.67	1.59
Sugar cane	Raw Sugar			
>1 Million Tons Per Year				
Kenya	−0.07	0.04	1.44	0.52
United Republic of Tanzania	−0.01	−0.01	1.73	0.41
Malawi	−0.01	0.09	2.51	0.60
Cameroon	−0.01	0.01	4.49	1.70
<1 Million Tons Per Year				
Zambia	−0.03	--	2.06	0.52
Ghana	−0.07	−0.04	1.84	1.44
Mali	−0.02	−0.02	2.31	1.17

[a]For wheat, world representative price in United States Gulf Ports.
[b]For sugar, producer price of sugar cane converted to raw sugar equivalent. World representative price refers to Caribbean sugar traded in New York.
– 5,000 tons

Source: IMF, *International Financial Statistics Yearbook 1984* (Washington: D.C., 1984).

domestic wheat production. In the event, farm prices were very close to the import unit value level in 1966–1968 except for Cameroon, and the ratio had increased in Ethiopia, Zambia, and Cameroon by 1979–1981 although it had fallen in Kenya and the United Republic of Tanzania. The ratio of farm price to a world representative price was above 1.20 in all countries except Cameroon (a very small producer) in 1966–1968 and was still around or above this level in 1979–1981. Thus the empirical evidence suggests that the price must have been at or around the equilibrium level throughout the period in most countries.

Sugar

Growth in sugar production has been so rapid in several African countries as a result of major investments in this area that, although all eight countries studied were net importers of sugar at the beginning of the period, by 1979–1981 the four countries with the highest production growth rates (Kenya, Malawi, Cameroon, and Zambia) were net exporters and the import deficit situation in the other three countries had improved. In this case we might expect to see the ratios of producer price to world representative price fall in export surplus countries as the equilibrium price would now be the export unit value minus the costs of marketing and transporting sugar from farms to ports. The empirical evidence in general supports this (Table 6.3), with falls from well above 1.00 to around 0.5 to 0.6 in Kenya, Malawi, and Zambia. However, in Cameroon, although the ratio fell substantially, it was still 1.7 in 1979–1981 and in the United Republic of Tanzania the rate fell to only 0.4 even though the country was a marginal importer in 1979–1981. It is conceivable that high domestic transport costs within the United Republic of Tanzania could help explain this result.

Summary

The overwhelming impression gained from this exercise is that there is very little evidence of producer prices being depressed below the equilibrium level at the official exchange rate as far as tradeable foodstuffs are concerned except, perhaps, for groundnuts. Of course, in some countries these results may mask the implicit taxation of food crops arising from overvaluation. One noticeable feature that does emerge, however, is that in countries like Ghana, which allowed their currency to become massively overvalued, the ratio of producer price to world representative price becomes extremely large, reflecting the extent to which it has been necessary to raise nominal prices (and in most but not all instances real prices) to prevent a decline in domestic food production. Ironically, massive overvaluation, which some would argue is a device to depress domestic food prices, has led to large increases in producer prices for foodstuffs as the foreign exchange shortages intensify.

The Real Producer Price of Cash Crop Products

We have seen that in a majority of cases, the real price of food crops has increased over the past decade. Can the same be said for cash crop prices? In Table 6.4 the compound annual percentage rate of growth in the producer price of coffee, cocoa, and seed cotton over the period 1968–1980 has been examined for all countries with complete price data over this period. Although producer prices tended to fluctuate from year to year it can be seen that the trend of the real producer price of coffee was downwards in all major producing countries except Kenya. The real producer price of seed cotton also fell in six of the seven largest producing countries. However, the price of cocoa fell in only one of the four major producing countries. The overall impression gained, then, is that the real price of cash crops declined. The real gross income from cash crops also fell in several instances.

Producer Prices and World Prices for Cash Crops

The trends in real prices for cash crops shown in Table 6.4 also influence the direction of change in the ratio of producer price to the export unit value or world representative price, a positive compound annual percentage growth rate tending to be associated with an increase in the ratio of producer price to export unit value (or world representative price in the case of cotton). As discussed in Appendix 1, it is difficult to ascertain from the ratio of producer price to export unit value whether producers are being deliberately "taxed" unless information is available on the level of domestic marketing costs. Moreover, this analysis does not reveal the extent of implicit taxation through overvaluation (see Appendix 1). However, some possible pointers can be gleaned from the overall level of the ratio and trends over time.

Coffee

A simple average of the ratios for the three years 1968–1970 reveals extremely high ratios in Ghana (0.98) and Kenya (0.93). Both of these may be misleading. The high figure for Ghana might be explained by the extremely low figure for export unit values recorded in the FAO statistics for early years, while it is suspected that the Kenya data reflect the average payment to cooperative societies rather than the actual farm gate price. The next highest ratios were in the United Republic of Tanzania (0.81) and the Central Afri-

Table 6.4 Trends in Cash Crop Pricing and Production, 1968–80

Countries Ranked by Production Level 1978–80 Average Per Year	Compound Annual Percentage Change 1968–80 in: Real Producer Price	Compound Annual Percentage Change 1968–80 in: Real Export Value	Simple Average Ratio of Producer Price to Unit Export Value 1968–70	Simple Average Ratio of Producer Price to Unit Export Value 1978–80	Compound Annual Percentage Change 1968–80 in: Production (tons)	Compound Annual Percentage Change 1968–80 in: Real Gross Income
Coffee						
>50,000 Tons Clean Coffee						
Côte-d'Ivoire	-1.0	2.3	0.51	0.44	-0.1ns	-1.1
Cameroon	-1.1	3.1	0.67	0.46	1.6	0.5
Zaire	-24.4	-2.0	0.56	0.06	2.6	-21.8
Kenya	5.6	4.9	0.93	1.01	5.8	11.4
Madagascar	-1.7	5.6	0.58	0.31	2.5	0.8
10,000 to 50,000 Tons						
United Republic of Tanzania	-1.8ns	5.1	0.81	0.47	-0.1	-1.4
Central African Republic	-10.0	3.1	0.71	0.23	6.1	-3.9
<10,000 Tons Per Year						
Sierra Leone	8.9	9.1	0.55	0.59	3.0ns	11.9
Zimbabwe	-0.3	5.3	0.60	0.38	33.9	33.6
Nigeria	1.6	0.0ns	0.56	0.69	0.4ns	2.0
Ghana	-10.0	-3.5	0.98	0.45	-10.5	-20.5
Malawi	0.5ns	8.1	0.48	0.27	21.9	22.4
Cocoa						
>100,000 Tons Per Year						
Côte-d'Ivoire	2.0	2.5	0.42	0.43	7.7	9.7
Ghana	-7.0	-5.5	0.41	0.34	-4.0	-11.0
Nigeria	3.3	-3.6	0.33	0.88	-3.7	-0.4
Cameroon	1.9	3.1	0.39	0.43	-0.7ns	1.2
<10,000 Tons Per Year						
Sierra Leone	11.0	8.5	0.46	0.66	3.5	14.5
Zaire	2.4	-0.2ns	0.21	0.34	-3.6	-1.2
Madagascar	-5.0	4.4	0.14	0.07	6.4	1.4
United Republic of Tanzania	-1.5	3.5	0.45	0.32	12.2	10.7

Table 6.4 Continued

	Compound Annual Percentage Change 1968–80 in Real:			Simple Average Ratio of Producer Price to the:				Compound Annual Percentage Change 1968–80 in:	
				Unit Export Value		World Representative Price			
	Producer Price	Export Unit Value	World Representative Price	1968–70	1978–80	1968–70	1978–80	Producer (tons)	Real Gross Income
Seed Cotton									
>100,000 tons									
United Republic of Tanzania	-0.9	-0.9 ns	-0.3 ns	0.56	1.04	0.53	0.50	-1.4 ns	-2.3
Zimbabwe	2.2	4.4	2.8	1.07	0.89	0.80	0.75	5.1	7.3
Côte–d'Ivoire	-1.7	-0.9 ns	-2.6	0.61	0.61	0.48	0.53	12.2	10.5
Nigeria	-1.5	na	-5.9	na	na	0.58	0.85	-1.1 ns	-2.6
25,000 to 100,000 tons									
Cameroon	-3.4	0.4 ns	-1.6	0.58	0.42	0.43	0.35	1.7 ns	-1.7
Burkina Faso	-1.6	1.0	0.7 ns	0.60	0.51	0.45	0.38	9.2	7.6
Central African Republic	-2.5	-9.7	-0.9 ns	0.54	1.12	0.45	0.35	-6.1	-9.7
Kenya	1.8	-1.3	0.4 ns	0.49	0.68	0.53	0.63	6.4	9.2
Zaire	7.7	na	-7.2	na	na	0.25	1.23	-6.0	1.7
Malawi	0.1 ns	3.2	2.2	0.58	0.42	0.45	0.38	5.4	5.5
Senegal	0.7 ns	-1.1 ns	-1.4 ns	0.31	0.39	0.28	0.35	9.4	10.1
<25,000 tons									
Zambia	4.1	na	1.5	na	na	0.68	0.83	7.3	11.4
Ghana	-7.3	na	-11.6	na	na	0.63	0.73	41.5	34.2
Niger	-5.5	-1.5	-2.0	1.69	1.20	1.05	0.80	-4.2	-9.7
Somalia	-5.3	na	-1.7 ns	na	na	0.88	0.58	1.5 ns	-3.8

Analysis of the Annual Rates of Growth in Real Price

	Negative	Positive	Positive ns	Negative ns
Coffee	7	3	1	1
Cocoa	3	5	–	–
Cotton	10	4	2	–

Analysis of the Annual Rates of Growth in Real Gross Income

	Negative	Positive
Coffee	4	8
Cocoa	3	5
Cotton	6	10

ns: not significant   na: not available

can Republic (0.71). Most other ratios were in the 0.5 to 0.7 range but Malawi (the smallest producer) had a ratio of only 0.48.

Over the period 1968–1970 to 1978–1980, the annual average rate of growth of real export unit values for coffee was positive for all countries except Zaire and Ghana. However, the ratio of producer price to export unit value has risen only in the three countries with positive growth rates in real price (Sierra Leone, Kenya, Nigeria). In all other countries where the real producer price had declined, the ratio was below 0.5 in 1978–1980 and below 0.3 in Malawi, the Central African Republic, and Zaire. Unless the costs of marketing have risen dramatically over the past decade, the inference must be that coffee producers, even if not "taxed" in 1968–1970 were being "taxed" quite substantially in 1978–1980 in the years immediately after the coffee boom. This "taxation" may not have been direct taxation by the government but might have resulted from a variety of charges imposed by marketing agencies, etc.

Cocoa

In 1968–1970, the highest ratios of producer price to world price were in Sierra Leone and the United Republic of Tanzania, but were only 0.46 and 0.45 respectively. Unless there are considerably higher marketing and processing costs associated with cocoa than coffee, this suggests that there was already considerable "taxation" of cocoa producers in this earlier period. Between 1968–1970 and 1978–1980 the real producer price rose in five countries and the ratio of producer price to export value rose in these countries, while falling in the three countries with real price declines. Even so, apart from Nigeria, with a ratio of 0.88, and Sierra Leone (0.66), the ratio in all other countries remained below 0.45.

Cotton

The irregularity of cotton exports from several cotton producing countries led to the producer price being compared with a world representative price (Mexican, St.Middling 1 1/16 inch c.i.f. N. Europe) as well as to the unit export value (where regular series were available). Because of the varying qualities of cotton produced in different countries, and the need to convert the producer price of seed cotton to a cotton lint equivalent, the actual coefficients may not be too reliable as indicators of the share of the world price accruing to producers. The discussion below refers mainly to the world representative price.

In 1968–1970, of the four largest producers, Zimbabwe had the highest ratio (0.80), followed by Nigeria (0.58), the United Republic of Tanzania (0.53), and Côte–d'Ivoire (0.43). The majority of countries had ratios in the

0.4 to 0.6 range. The real world price fell in most countries, and so those countries with an increase in real producer price experienced an increase in the ratio of producer price to representative price. By 1979–1980, the ratio in Nigeria had risen to 0.85, followed by Zimbabwe (0.75), Côte–d'Ivoire (0.53), the United Republic of Tanzania (0.50). However, whereas in 1968–1970 only Senegal had a ratio below 0.4, in 1978–1980 five countries were in this position. Part of the low ratio in Malawi, Burkina Faso, and the Central African Republic may have been associated with the high transport costs associated with a bulky product like cotton lint. This contention is supported by the evidence in the Appendix, Table 6.5, where the NPCs for cotton are considerably higher than the ratio of actual producer price to unit export values. The only major discrepancy between trends in unit export values and world representative prices occurs in the Central African Republic where the real unit export value declines dramatically.

Summary

There is evidence both that the real producer price for cash crops declined in several countries, and that the ratio of producer price to export values, already well below 1.00 in many instances, declined still further over the years. This tends to confirm the allegation that export crops have been heavily taxed. There are, of course, many exceptions in regard to individual countries and/or commodities, but the broad trend is sufficiently marked to stand in contrast with that for foodstuffs for which real producer prices rose in a majority of cases and the ratio of producer prices to world representative prices was both much higher and rising. These findings are consistent with our argument in Chapter 5 that it is very difficult for most African countries to control food prices effectively and suggest that the Berg Report was wrong in its suggestions regarding the deliberate suppression of food crop prices.

• NOTES •

1. World Bank, *Accelerated Development in Sub-Saharan Africa* (Washington, D.C., 1981).
2. FAO, *Food Balance Sheets 1975–77 Average and Per Capita Food Supplies* (Rome: FAO, 1980).

Appendix 1: METHODOLOGICAL ISSUES
INVOLVED IN PRICE ANALYSIS

Data Sources

The empirical evidence presented here has been derived mainly from three interrelated exercises. Our first examination of the problem was contained in a paper written in mid-1983.[1] Subsequently, one of the authors assisted FAO in the preparation of a paper on agricultural price policies in Africa[2] and some of the data presented here was prepared for that paper. More detailed analysis for a subset of sub-Saharan African countries has recently been carried out as part of the FAO study on agricultural price policies.[3]

The price series available for the first two exercises were mainly the official FAO producer prices series, which are compiled from information made available to FAO by member governments through the production questionnaire or obtained from official country publications. The first exercise used data published by FAO in 1982[4] and mainly related to the period 1969–1980. The second exercise, however, was conducted with direct access to the FAO Interlinked Computerized Storage and Processing System of Food and Agricultural Commodity Data (ICS). Attention was concentrated on countries with complete price data from 1968 to 1980; for some countries there were minor revisions to data available for the first exercise. For the third exercise, price data collected by the World Bank, IMF, official country sources, etc., were investigated in an attempt to improve the quality and range of the FAO data. This again means that some of the data used in the second exercise were modified by the time the third exercise was conducted. Moreover, this later exercise was conducted over a longer time span, 1966–1981. None of these region-wide exercises incorporated some of the more recent dramatic changes in prices indicated in the case studies in the next chapter. In this sense, they are historical records relating to what is thought to have happened in the 1970s.

Data Limitations

Despite attempts to improve the data, there are obvious limitations to them. For instance, for several countries the price series provided by governments appear to refer to official producer prices or support prices, and these do not always adequately reflect farm gate prices. To a large extent this problem is understandable. A large volume of food crop output is not sold to official agencies, and the price obtained varies considerably depending on local supply and demand conditions. The data collection services available in most countries are simply inadequate to collect this information. Furthermore, where information is collected, it is often at a "depot" and various deductions may be required to arrive at the actual farm gate price.

An identical problem concerns selection of the retail prices of food items. Not only may such prices vary considerably from one part of the country to another, but also in any given area there may be an official retail price as well as a series of prices in the semi-legal, open, or parallel markets. In some countries the food prices in the cost-of-living index are derived from the actual prices in several retail markets. In such situations the consumer food prices may approximate some sort of average of the official and free market prices. In other cases, however, the food prices may refer to the official retail prices, which may, however, give a quite misleading picture of the actual level and changes in prices of food items.

Similar reservations have to be expressed concerning the production data. For many African countries and for a variety of crops the crop reporting services do not have the resources to record areas or yield accurately, and the FAO data, although in most instances the best available, may involve a considerable margin of error.

The Estimation of Real Producer and Consumer Prices

There are also problems in data interpretation. For most purposes, it is more desirable to conduct analyses on real or deflated prices than on actual or nominal prices. One of our main concerns is with producers' real purchasing power, and for many countries the most readily available and consistent series to deflate nominal or actual producer prices is the consumer price index published in the ILO Yearbook of Labour Statistics or the IMF consumer price index[5] which is derived mainly from the ILO statistics. These series were used as price deflators in the first two exercises. The main difference is that in some instances the IMF provides a chain-linked series in circumstances where the ILO has decided that the changes in data coverage or weightings are too great to justify linking. For most countries, the ILO and IMF consumer prices series refer to the cost of living in urban areas and often to middle-income families. Thus they are not ideally suited to considering the purchasing power of commodities produced in rural areas by low-income farmers or foodstuffs consumed in rural areas. Certain items such as house rent, an important component in the cost-of-living index for urban households, are largely irrelevant for most rural households. Similar considerations apply to the use of a middle-income cost-of-living index for deflating the price of items consumed by low-income urban households. The consumer prices for individual food items and, therefore, the food component of the cost-of-living index, are generally based on prices for both imported and local foods. This point is particularly relevant when comparing the movements in, say, the consumer and producer prices of individual food items.

In view of the preceding remarks, it is clear that the estimates of changes in the real price of food and farm products may not always be accurate. The point applies, a fortiori, to comparisons across countries.

The Measurement of Price Changes over Time

Throughout the report the statistic used to measure price changes over time is the annual average percentage change per year derived from an exponential trend fitted to time series data by regression. This has the advantage over a growth rate calculated using end years, or three-year average end periods, of taking all years into account. However, it suffers from the disadvantage that the value so derived can be misleading in situations in which, for instance, the price rises to a peak in the middle of time series and then declines again. No single measure is ever perfect but on balance we decided that the exponential growth rate suited our purposes best.

The Comparison of Domestic and World Prices

One of the major reasons for undertaking the empirical analysis of price trends is to determine the extent to which domestic producer prices have been distorted by government intervention. The usual yardstick for this comparison is the price obtained for a similar product obtainable on world markets. There are, however, two major problems in making this comparison. The first stems from the existence of transport, marketing, and processing costs. The second relates to the choice of the appropriate exchange rate to use in converting prices quoted in foreign currencies to domestic currency terms.

Transport, Marketing, and Processing Costs

For commodities a country is both producing and importing, the question we have to resolve is, "How much could be paid to the farmer at the farm gate to make his product just competitive with the imported article in satisfying domestic consumer needs?" To establish this equilibrium price one would start with the appropriate international price converted at the official exchange rate and *add* costs, insurance, and ocean freight to give the c.i.f. price. To this would be *added* handling and transport costs and marketing margins from the border to the domestic market. The equilibrium price for the producer at the farm gate would then be this market price for the imported product *minus* transport, processing and handling costs, and marketing margins from the farm to the market.

In symbols, the producer equilibrium price for an imported commodity is thus:

$$x + a + b - c$$

where x is the world representative price converted at the official exchange rate;

a represents international transport and marketing charges

b represents transport and marketing charges from port to domestic market;

c represents transport, processing, and marketing charges from farm gate to domestic market.

For commodities a country is exporting, to establish the farm gate price that would just make the item competitive on world markets one would again start with the appropriate international price. However, this time one would *deduct* ocean freight, costs, and insurance to give the f.o.b. border price and *deduct* transport, processing and handling costs, and marketing margins from the farm to the border. In symbols:

$$x - a - b - c$$

The ratio of the actual farm gate price (P) to these adjusted border prices (*producer equilibrium prices*) is one measure of the Nominal Protection Coefficient (*NPC*). Obviously, a ratio of 1.00 would indicate that at the official exchange rate the farmer is obtaining the equivalent of the world price and, in this sense, is being neither "taxed" nor subsidized. Movements in this ratio over time also indicate whether the actual producer price is moving towards or away from its equilibrium value.

Ideally, we would have liked to estimate the NPCs for a variety of commodities and countries over a range of years. However, collecting the information necessary for these calculations is extremely exacting and time-consuming, and well beyond the resources of this study. Indeed, although NPCs have been calculated by several organizations for individual commodities and countries for isolated years, there are, to the best of our knowledge, very few studies in which NPCs have been carefully calculated for a run of years.[6] Some estimates from the FAO pricing policy study are shown in Table 6.5 in this appendix.

We have had to rely on a much cruder measure, the ratio of the actual producer price (P) to the average annual per unit value of imports ($x + a$) or exports ($x - a$), or where trade flows or data were inadequate for a meaningful estimate, a representative annual price from one of the major international markets for the commodity (x). Although this ratio is relatively easy to

Table 6.5 Some Comparisons of the Ratio of Actual Producer
Price to Import (Export) Unit Values and Nominal Protection
Coefficients

Country and Commodity	Year	Ratio of Actual Producer Price to Import (Export) Unit Value Crude	Nominal Protection Coefficient Corrected
Food Crops with Import Deficit			
Rice			
Côte–d'Ivoire	1984 (State)	0.95	1.99
Kenya	1982/83	0.58	0.67
	(Basmati variety)		
Senegal	1982	0.61	0.74
United Republic	1982/83	0.59	0.85
of Tanzania	1983/84	0.61	1.13
Food Crops with Export Surplus			
Rice			
Malawi	1977 (Salima area)	0.70	2.19
Groundnuts			
Malawi	1977	0.42	0.46
Mali	1978/79	0.31	0.43
Sudan	1982/83	0.69	1.00
Cash Crops with Export Surplus			
Cotton			
Côte–d'IVoire	1982/83	0.53	0.82
Kenya	1981	0.76	1.00
	1976/77	0.25	0.30
Mali	1978/79	0.43	0.61
Sudan	1982/83	0.66	0.77

Source: FAO, *Agricultural Price Policies* (Rome: FAO, C85/19 August 1985), Table 1,
pp. 113–114.

calculate, it is much harder to interpret than a properly calculated NPC,
where a value of less than 1.00 implies taxation, and a value of greater than
1.00 implies subsidization.

For instance, for export commodities, if the producer is being paid the
equilibrium price, the ratio P/x must clearly be less than 1.00, the actual level
depending on the relative importance of marketing and transport costs to
the world representative price. For imported commodities, whether this
ratio P/x is greater or less than 1.00 when the producer receives the equilibrium price depends on whether a and b combined are greater or lesser than
c. In other words, if it costs more to transport and market the domestic product from the farm gate to the final consumer than it costs to transport and
market the imported product, then this ratio will be below 1.00. (The United
Republic of Tanzania offers good examples of this because many of the more
productive food-producing areas are on the periphery of the country while

Dar es Salaam, the main urban consumption center, is also the major port.) Similarly, if it costs more to transport and market the imported product to the final consumer than it costs to market the domestic product from the farm gate to the final consumer, then a ratio of more than 1.00 between the gross producer price and world price is quite consistent with the farmer's receiving the equilibrium price.

If the ratio of the equilibrium price to the world price can take on a wide range of values, how can we interpret the ratio of an actual producer price to a representative world price? Obviously, only the broadest generalizations can be made. The safest is that if the ratio exceeds 1.00 when a country has an exportable surplus, producers are obviously being protected at the official exchange rate. Similarly, if a country moves over a period of a few years from exporting a surplus to importing to compensate for a domestic deficit, then if actual producer prices reflect the equilibrium price, we would expect the ratio of the producer price to the world price to rise, with a proviso that marketing and transport costs retain a relatively constant relationship with the world price. Again, a comparison of the actual producer price to a world representative price in countries thought to have similar marketing and transport costs can rank countries roughly in order of approximation to the equilibrium producer price at the official exchange rate. However, with the possibility of all four variables—x, a, b, and c—varying between countries or over time, any conclusions reached using the ratio of actual producer price to world price need to be treated cautiously.

The Use of the Official Exchange Rate in Comparing Domestic and International Prices

Another problem relates to the choice of an appropriate exchange rate when comparing domestic and international prices. In Chapter 6 the world price has been converted at the official exchange rate and then converted to a real domestic price by deflating by the domestic rate of inflation. The real domestic producer price has then been compared with this real world price. However, a common tendency in many sub-Saharan countries during the 1970s was not to adjust the exchange rate even though the domestic rate of inflation exceeded that of the country's major trading partners. As a result, even though the domestic producer price might rise as a proportion of the world price at the official exchange rate, its real international purchasing power might fall. In this sense, there is an implicit taxation of producers in addition to any explicit taxation that might occur.

For example, assume world inflation of 10 percent and domestic inflation of 20 percent. If the world price of a commodity last year was $100 per ton, its price would now have to be $110 to keep its real price unchanged. Assume the domestic exchange rate last year was 100 naira = $1; i.e., the domestic value of one ton of the commodity last year was 10,000 naira, the exchange rate would now have to change to $(1.2/1.1) \times 100 = 109$ naira = \$1 to maintain the real domestic value of 1 ton of the commodity, i.e., \$110 × 109 = 12,000 naira, which with 20 percent inflation is equivalent to 10,000 naira in the previous year. If the exchange rate had remained unchanged at 100 naira = \$1, the domestic value would now be 11,000 naira, which would have a real domestic purchasing power of only 9,167 naira at last year's prices; i.e., there has been a loss of 8.3 percent purchasing power. Assume now that the government pays the producer 50 percent of the world price. His return would increase from 5,000 to 5,500 naira at the official exchange rate, compared with the 5,995 naira he would have obtained at the "purchasing power parity" exchange rate; i.e., there is an implicit taxation of $(5,000/5,995) \times 100 = 8.3$ percent in addition to the explicit taxation of 50 percent.

Because of this it is sometimes argued that a "purchasing power" exchange rate should be used in comparing domestic and international prices. We have not done this in Chapter 6 for two reasons. First, it is by no means obvious that an equilibrium exchange rate would necessarily coincide with that obtained by a purchasing power parity calculation. Secondly, it is rather naive to assume that domestic producer prices would remain unchanged if the exchange rate were adjusted. In this sense, the implicit level of taxation is hypothetical. Nevertheless, in many countries a considerable degree of distortion was undoubtedly introduced into agricultural pricing in the 1970s through the use of overvalued exchange rates. Some indication of this can be obtained from the index of overvaluation described below.

The Index of Overvaluation

An index of overvaluation is used in Chapter 7. This was calculated for one of the FAO studies[7] (see Appendix 1, Table 6.5, this chapter). The parity ex-

Table 6.6 Indices of Purchasing Power Parity Overvaluation, 1978–80 Simple Average with 1970 = 1.00

Ghana	3.96	United Republic of Tanzania	1.42
Zaire	2.84	Kenya	1.42
Nigeria	2.43	Burkina Faso	1.40
Côte–d'Ivoire	1.87	Madagascar	1.40
Niger	1.82	Zambia	1.24
Cameroon	1.75	Malawi	1.15
Senegal	1.68	Zimbabwe	1.11
Somalia	1.67	Sierra Leone	1.05
Central African Republic	1.66		

Source: FAO, *Agricultural Price Policies in Africa* (Rome: FAO, ARC/84/4, May 1984), Table 2, p. 11.

change rate for each year was calculated as:

$$
\begin{array}{l} \text{1970 exchange rate} \\ \text{in US\$ per unit} \\ \text{domestic currency} \end{array} \times \frac{\text{United States consumer price index (1970 = 100)}}{\text{Country consumer price index (1970 = 100)}}
$$

The official exchange rate in any one year was then divided by the parity exchange rate to give the degree of overvaluation on a base of 1970 = 1.00.

• NOTES •

1. D. Ghai and L. Smith, *Food Policy and Equity in Sub-Saharan Africa*, Mimeographed World Employment Programme Research Working Paper WEP 10-6/WP55 (Geneva: ILO, 1983). Paper presented at a conference on Accelerating Agricultural Production for Sub-Saharan Africa, Zimbabwe, August–September 1983, organized by the International Food Policy Research Institute.

2. FAO, *Agricultural Price Policies in Africa*, Thirteenth FAO Regional Conference for Africa, Harare, Zimbabwe, 16–25 July 1984 (Rome: FAO, ARC/84/4, May 1984), p. 33

3. FAO, *Agricultural Price Policies*, Twenty-third Session of the FAO Conference, Rome, 9–28 November 1985 (Rome: FAO, C85/19 August 1985), p. 117.

4. See FAO, *Statistics on Prices Received by Farmers*, Statistics Division, Economic Social Policy Department (Rome: FAO, 1982).

5. IMF, *International Financial Statistics*, Supplement on Price Statistics, Supplement Series No. 2 (Washington, D.C., 1981).

6. One reason for this neglect may be that the accurate measurement of marketing costs can be quite complicated, although a manual setting out a methodology for dealing with the complexities is available. See L. D. Smith, *A Methodology for Measuring Marketing Costs and Margins for Foodstuffs in Developing Countries* (Rome: FAO, AMS, May 1981).

7. FAO, *Agricultural Price Policies in Africa*, pp. 10–11.

Appendix 2: AN INTERCOUNTRY COMPARISON OF PRODUCER PRICES

It would be useful to be able to compare real producer price levels for the same agricultural product in different countries. Producers in two countries could be said to have the same real price if the purchasing power of a ton of the product were the same in both countries. This cannot be achieved by converting the different currencies to a single numeraire currency using the official exchange rate if the exchange rates themselves do not reflect the domestic purchasing power of the currency. (In this respect it should be remembered that currency exchange rates tend to reflect supply and demand in traded goods and finance markets whereas consumer purchasing power is concerned with traded and non-traded goods.)

Fortunately, a means of making at least approximate international comparisons of the real purchasing power of producer prices is now available as a spin-off of the United Nations International Comparison Project (ICP). Summers and Heston[1] have recently interpolated estimates of real product for 124 countries for the period 1960–1980 from the actual results of the thirty-four benchmark countries examined in Phase III of the ICP. In the process they have calculated the purchasing power parity of the domestic currency per unit numeraire currency (the U.S. dollar) for final consumption purposes (PPP^c). Given a domestic producer price for a commodity, P^d, its current purchasing power in international currency units, PPi, can be expressed as

$$PPi = \frac{Pij^d t}{PPP^c jt}$$

where $Pij^d t$ refers to the price of commodity i in country j in year t in domestic currency terms. To convert this current purchasing power to real terms an appropriate deflator is the consumption expenditure deflator for the United States, as it offers both the numeraire currency and country.

This approach and methodology has been used to compare producer prices in terms of constant 1975 international units for thirteen countries. We have termed these "real purchasing power prices" (RPP). It must be stressed that these RPPs are tentative, especially for the sub-Saharan African countries, partly because of the weak nature of much of the original national income data and partly because of the interpolation technique used to generate the PPP^cs.

• AN INTERCOUNTRY COMPARISON OF FOOD CROP PRICES •

Providing the methodology underlying the RPP analysis is sound, a low RPP for a commodity may emerge when a country has a strong natural advantage in the production of that commodity. Thus low RPPs may be consistent with a sustained exportable surplus of a crop. On the other hand, a low RPP may signify that producers are being implicitly or explicitly taxed, and if resources are mobile we would in this case expect to see continuing low RPPs associated with a declining output of the crop in question. Equally, high RPPs will usually signify inefficient or protected producers who are receiving a return in excess of that obtaining on the world market. Using these criteria, the results of the analysis for individual crops will be examined.

Maize

In Table 6.7 the countries have been ranked in descending order of the estimated RPP of a ton of product in 1966–1968. For maize, the RPP per ton was
highest in Ghana and Nigeria at around $350 per ton. At the other end of the
spectrum four countries—Sierra Leone, the United Republic of Tanzania,
Mali, and Malawi—had an RPP per ton of less than one-half of this figure,
with the other countries with RPPs in the $180–260 range.

By 1979–1981 the ranking of the seven countries with the highest RPPs
had hardly changed except for the decline in the RPP in Kenya. But the rise
in RPP in Ghana was much more rapid than in any other country, so that by
1979–1981 its RPP of $612 per ton was almost 70 percent higher than that in
the next two countries, Ethiopia and Nigeria. It may be noted, however, that
this gap is much less than that implied by considering relative producer
prices converted at the official exchange rate. Although the RPP rose in most
of the countries with a high RPP in 1966–1968, it fell in four of the five countries with the lowest RPPs in 1966–1968, making the spread of RPPs even
wider than before. The exception was the United Republic of Tanzania,
where the RPP may have risen in response to the continuing and increasing
import deficit.

Rice (Paddy)

in 1966–1968 Nigeria had an RPP for rice (paddy) 80 percent higher than
that for the next two countries, Zambia and Senegal. The two countries with
the lowest RPPs for maize, Malawi and Mali, also had the lowest RPPs for rice
(paddy), at below $200 per ton. Thus, there was a wider spread in RPP rice
prices than there was for maize. Over the period 1966–1968 to 1979–1981,
however, there was a much greater change in the relative positions of RPPs
than for maize. The three countries with the highest RPPs in 1966–1968 all
experienced price falls while most other countries had increases in RPP.
There were substantial increases in Cameroon and Ghana and a decline in
Nigeria, so that in 1979–1981 these three countries had RPPs in the $570-640
per ton range. There was a considerable gap between RPPs in these countries and the six countries with RPPs in the $300-380 range. At the bottom
end, the RPPs in Malawi and Mali were below $200.

Wheat

In 1966–1968 three of the five wheat producing countries had RPPs in the
$350-400 range, with Cameroon, a very small producer, having an RPP of

Table 6.7 A Comparison of the Real Purchasing Power (RPP)
of the Producer Price of Food Crops

Countries Ranked by RPP Value 1966–68	Simple Average of RPP of Producer Price (Dollars per Ton at 1975 Constant Prices) 1966–78	1979–81	RPP Ranking 1979-81	Compound Annual Percentage Rate of Growth in RPP 1966-81
Maize				
Ghana	369	612	1	6.09
Nigeria	347	364	3	–0.32 ns
Ethiopia	261	366	2	2.39
Cameroon	246	354	4	2.86
Niger	237	320	5	2.42
Kenya	231	175	9	–0.89 ns
Senegal	205	269	6	3.19
Zambia	199	219	7	0.80
Côte–d'Ivoire	185	148	10	–1.38
Sierra Leone	168	104	13	–3.32
United Republic of Tanzania	166	190	8	2.17
Mali	154	147	11	–0.52 ns
Malawi	140	109	12	–1.12
Rice Paddy				
Nigeria	771	620	2	–2.16
Zambia	425	349	5	–0.80 ns
Senegal	404	299	9	–1.27
Sierra Leone	349	377	4	0.68
Niger	306	320	6	0.34
Kenya	301	295	10	0.47 ns
Côte–d'Ivoire	278	314	7	2.30
Ghana	276	572	3	6.01
United Republic of Tanzania	271	301	8	0.32 ns
Cameroon	217	638	1	8.94
Malawi	190	181	11	–0.64 ns
Mali	160	167 [a]	12	na
Wheat				
Ethiopia	399	476	1	0.93
Kenya	366	307	4	–0.71
United Republic of Tanzania	358	280	5	–1.36
Zambia	285	448	2	4.88
Cameroon	183	353	3	5.49
Sugar Cane				
Cameroon	80	76	1	–0.39 ns
Mali	45	36 [a]	2	na
Malawi	36	31	4	–0.42 ns
Ghana	34	32 [b]	3	na
Zambia	30	25	6	–1.48
Kenya	29	27	5	–0.01 ns
United Republic of Tanzania	25	19	7	–1.40

only $180. RPPs rose in four of the five countries over the period 1966–1968 to 1979–1981, falling only in the United Republic of Tanzania. As a result the RPP in Ethiopia and Zambia had risen to $450-480 in 1979–1981 but was only $280 in Tanzania.

Sugar Cane

Cameroon's RPP for sugar cane was out of line with those of other countries, in both 1966–1968 and 1979–1981. Interestingly, the countries with the next highest RPPs were Mali and Malawi, which had the lowest RPP prices for maize and rice (paddy). The United Republic of Tanzania, already the country with the lowest RPP in 1966–1968, was one of the few countries to experience a price fall, so that by 1979–1981 the RPP per ton was substantially below those of other countries.

Table 6.7 Continued

Countries Ranked by RPP Value 1966–68	Simple Average of RPP of Producer Price (Dollars per Ton at 1975 Constant Prices)		RPP Ranking 1978–80	Compound Annual Percentage Rate of Growth in RPP 1968–80
	1968–70	1978–80		
Groundnuts				
Ghana	614	1674	1	10.3
United Republic of Tanzania	552	775	2	4.2
Cameroon	469	673	5	3.6
Kenya	441	350	7	−1.9
Zambia	407	747	4	7.2
Sierra Leone	360	308	8	−2.2
Côte–d'Ivoire	302	144	11	−7.0
Senegal	279	323	8	2.3
Malawi	266	366	6	3.0
Nigeria	248	753	3	12.8
Niger	222	307	10	4.1

Analysis of the Rates of Growth in RPP

	Negative	Positive	Positive ns	Negative ns	na
Maize	3	7	--	3	
Rice paddy	2	5	2	2	1
Wheat	1	4	--	−	
Sugar cane	2	−	−	3	2

a1979 only.   ns: not significant
b1979–80 only.   na: not available

Groundnuts

Information on groundnuts was available only for the period 1968–1980. At the start of the period the significant exporters of groundnuts, Senegal, Malawi, Nigeria, and Niger, had the lowest RPP prices, between $280 and $220 per ton. This would be consistent with their competing on the world market. It might be noted that the ratio of farm prices to world representative price was in the range 0.38 to 0.57 for this to occur.

At the same time the RPP per ton in Ghana and the United Republic of Tanzania was more than double that in the exporting countries. As with other food crops, the RPP per ton rose rapidly in Ghana so that by 1978–1980 the RPP was around $1675 per ton whereas in Zambia, Nigeria, and the United Republic of Tanzania, where the price also rose rapidly, the RPP was in the $750-775 range. In Senegal, Malawi, and Niger, the net exporters in 1978–1980, the RPP was in the range $300-370, but in the Côte–d'Ivoire, the RPP had fallen to as little as $140 per ton.

Summary

In 1966–1968 no country except Ethiopia consistently appeared in the highest or lowest quartiles of RPP rankings for all crops produced in that country. However, the impression can be gained that RPP rankings tended to be highest overall in Ethiopia, Ghana, and Nigeria, and lowest in the Côte–d'Ivoire, Malawi, and Mali. By 1979–1981 Ghana, Nigeria, and Ethiopia appeared clearly as the countries with the highest RPPs for food crops, but Kenya had joined the Côte–d'Ivoire, Malawi, and Mali as the countries paying the lowest RPPs for food crops.

• AN INTERCOUNTRY COMPARISON OF CASH CROP PRICES •

As with food crops, an intercountry comparison of the real purchasing power of cash crop prices has been attempted for up to 13 countries for the period 1968–1980 (Appendix 2, Table 6.8).

Coffee

For coffee the results are available for eight countries. In RPP terms Kenya's producer price is well above that of any other country in both 1968–1970 and 1978–1980. This is due to a combination of the high quality arabica coffee grown in Kenya, the government policy of not taxing coffee revenue, and the possibility that the producer price is overstated. In 1968–1970 the United Republic of Tanzania, which grows arabica and robusta coffee, had the second highest producer price, but there was a slight decline over the years. The RPP price in Nigeria and Sierra Leone rose rapidly from a low base and by 1978–1980 was comparable with that in the United Republic of Tanzania. Côte–d'Ivoire and Malawi had low RPP prices throughout the entire period while the RPP price in Ghana fell extremely rapidly. As a result, the RPP price in Côte–d'Ivoire, Malawi, and Ghana in 1978–1980 was substantially below those of other countries.

Cocoa

RPP prices for cocoa are available for only six countries. In 1968–1970 the prices in all countries were in the $1100 to $1370 range, with the highest price in the United Republic of Tanzania and the lowest in Côte–d'Ivoire. However, over the years the RPP price rose rapidly in Nigeria and Sierra Leone (as it did for coffee), rose moderately in Côte–d'Ivoire and Cameroon and fell in the United Republic of Tanzania and Ghana. As a result, the RPP price in 1978–1980 was highest in Sierra Leone and Nigeria, in the range of $2500-2800, with $1500-1600 in Côte–d'Ivoire and Cameroon, and as low as $875 in Ghana.

Cotton

The quality differential may also be a factor in the RPPs for seed cotton with a wide range of prices in 1968–1970, the price of $1267 in Niger being substantially above that of other countries. At the other extreme the RPP price in Senegal was only $270. Seven other countries had RPP prices in the range $410 to $780. Between 1968–1970 and 1978–1980 the RPP price rose most rapidly in Zambia and declined most rapidly in Niger and Ghana. By 1978–1980 the RPP price was almost $850 in Zambia, was in the $700-760 range in Nigeria, Niger, and Kenya, and was below $500 in Ghana, Malawi, Côte–d'Ivoire and Senegal.

Summary

Taking the three cash crops together, the RPP price has fallen most rapidly in Ghana, and this has had an obvious impact on production (Table 6.8). RPP prices have been low in Côte–d'Ivoire and Malawi but have actually risen moderately over the period. As export volumes in these countries have in-

Table 6.8 The Real Purchasing Power (RPP) of the Producer Price of Cash Crops 1968–80

Countries Ranked by RPP Value 1968–70	Simple Average of RPP of Producer Price (Dollars per Ton at 1975 Constant Prices)		RPP Ranking 1978–80	Compound Annual Percentage Rate of Growth in RPP 1968–80
	1968–70	1978–80		
Coffee				
Kenya	4,226	6,102	1	5.1
United Republic of Tanzania	2,774	2,335	4	–0.8
Cameroon	2,087	1,874	5	–1.0
Ghana	1,635	832	8	–7.2
Nigeria	1,517	2,401	3	5.6
Sierra Leone	1,410	2,446	2	5.9
Côte–d'Ivoire	1,345	1,465	6	0.2 ns
Malawi	1,225	1,350	7	1.7
Cocoa				
United Republic of Tanzania	1,367	1,145	5	–0.1 ns
Nigeria	1,311	2,517	2	7.5
Sierra Leone	1,307	2,824	1	8.0
Cameroon	1,264	1,601	3	2.0
Ghana	1,250	875	6	–4.7
Côte–d'Ivoire	1,107	1,490	4	3.1
Cotton				
Niger	1,267	729	3	–5.6
Ghana	767	468	6	–4.4
Nigeria	666	755	2	2.3
Kenya	618	714	4	1.3
United Republic of Tanzania	589	549	5	–0.5 ns
Zambia	564	847	1	5.3
Côte–d'Ivoire	475	443	8	–0.6 ns
Malawi	410	464	7	1.3
Senegal	270	385	9	3.1

ns: not significant

creased, it may suggest that productivity improvements and other incentives are sufficient to encourage the development of cash crops even at these low prices.

• NOTE •

1. R. Summers and A. Heston, "Improved International Comparison of Real Product and Its Composition: 1950–80," *Review of Income and Wealth* (June 1984).

·7·

Agricultural Marketing
and Pricing:
Some Country Experiences

T he discussion in Chapter 5 focused on the role and limitations of pricing policy as an instrument of development planning in African countries. The preceding chapter examined various agricultural price trends in the light of this discussion. This chapter supplements the two preceding ones with a more detailed analysis of agricultural pricing and marketing in six African countries. The six countries comprise two each from eastern (Kenya and the United Republic of Tanzania), southern (Zambia and Malawi), and western Africa (Nigeria and Ghana). The period covered is 1968–1980 although wherever possible the data on more recent years are also presented to illustrate the impact of world recession and changes in policy. Although, as will be seen later, these countries display considerable diversity in the composition of agricultural output, the organization of production, the structure of marketing systems, and the evolution of agricultural prices, it is not claimed that they offer a representative sample of sub-Saharan Africa or that they illustrate all the major types of marketing systems and trends in agricultural prices encountered in Africa.

Within the limits of the data and information available, we describe briefly for each country some key features of the economy and the agricultural sector; the agricultural marketing and pricing system; the trends in real consumer and producer prices for main agricultural crops; and the main mechanisms and policy instruments determining the course of these prices. The final section compares and contrasts the individual country experiences and draws some general conclusions on agricultural price trends and policies in sub-Saharan Africa.

· KENYA ·

The per head income in Kenya was estimated at $390 in 1982, which places the country in about the middle among the sub-Saharan countries.[1] The gross national product (GNP) per head grew by 2.8 percent per year over the period 1960–1982, although since 1974 there has been a marked slowdown in the growth of the economy except for the short-lived commodity boom of 1977–1978. The country is predominantly agricultural, that sector accounting for 33 percent of GDP in 1982, having fallen from 38 percent in 1960. The share of industry, including manufacturing, has risen over the same period from 18 to 22 percent. The bulk of the population, 85 percent, live in rural areas (1982), and agriculture provides a livelihood for 78 percent of the labor force (1980). The two principal forms of agricultural production, of roughly equal importance in marketed agriculture, are plantations and large individual farms on one hand and smallholders on the other. The main agricultural crops are coffee, tea, sugar cane, wheat, maize, sisal, and pyrethrum.

Structure of Pricing and Marketing System

There is widespread regulation of the marketing and prices of agricultural commodities by the state marketing boards. The origins of state intervention in agricultural marketing and pricing go back to early colonial days.[2] The original motivation was to provide stable and remunerative returns to settler agriculture. The main focus was on food crops destined primarily for domestic consumption, namely maize and wheat. In the subsequent period, during and after the Second World War, marketing boards were created to cover all the major agricultural products, including livestock, dairy products, and export crops such as coffee, tea, pyrethrum, sisal, cotton, and horticultural products.

The objectives and roles of marketing boards vary from product to product and include recommendations on price fixing for producers and (where relevant) consumers, provision of marketing facilities, storage, processing, quality control, and sales overseas. With the exception of cotton, the marketing boards since independence have not been used for price or income stabilization for producers, nor to any significant extent to levy export taxes or build surpluses for reinvestment elsewhere, except for limited periods for certain crops. This, of course, does not imply that the levels at which prices were fixed did not result in an implicit taxation or subsidy for different sections of the population. The prices for crops handled by the boards are fixed by the government in consultation with the ministries and boards concerned. In general, the policy for export crops has been to let world prices determine the producer prices for growers. For food crops sold domestically, the criteria used in fixing prices are world prices, fair return to producers, the food situation in the country, and the impact on the cost of living.

The proportion of marketed output handled by the boards varies from one crop to another. In general it is realistic to assume that for export crops like coffee, tea, sisal, and pyrethrum, practically all the marketed output goes through the boards or bodies designated by them. For foodcrops the situation is more complex and also varies from year to year. For the two main foodstuffs, maize and wheat, the National Cereals and Produce Board (NCPB) has theoretically far-reaching control of marketing and pricing. The Board recommends to the government the level of producer, wholesale, and retail prices for maize and wheat. Through its licencees and agents, it is the sole legal buyer of these crops and is responsible for all imports and exports. As wheat is grown mostly on large farms and is milled by a relatively small number of millers, the Board is able to control most of the marketing. For maize, which is also grown by a large number of smallholders throughout the country, a considerable but variable amount of the crop bypasses the Board. It has been estimated that in the six years 1975–1976 to 1980–1981, the NCPB purchases amounted to about 20 percent of the estimated total production, of which probably 35 percent or more is marketed. The bulk of the NCPB sales take place in urban areas.[3]

Trends in Real Consumer and Producer Prices

Information on movements in consumer and producer prices for some important commodities in Kenya is summarized in Table 7.1. With respect to consumer food prices, a consistent food price index and consumer price

Table 7.1 Changes in Real Producer and Consumer Prices in Kenya

	Producer Prices			Consumer Prices	
	Annual Percentage Growth Rate				Annual Percentage Growth Rate
Commodity	1968–80	1968–83	Commodity		1968–80
Clean Coffee	5.6 ns	–0.7 ns			
Pyrethrum	–0.6 ns	–1.1 ns			
Seed Cotton	1.8	–0.5 ns			
Tea	–0.6 ns	–1.6 ns			
Maize	1.3 ns	–0.1 ns	Sugar		1.1 ns
Rice (Paddy)	2.1	–1.8 ns	Maize Meal		0.5 ns
Sugar Cane	1.0 ns	0.1 ns	Rice		–1.6
Wheat	0.8 ns	–1.0 ns	Wheat Flour		–2.2
			Bread		–3.5

ns: not significant at the 10% level.

Sources: FAO data tapes, ILO *Yearbook of Labour Statistics*, Country Statistical Abstracts.

index series is available only since 1972. By 1980 the food price index was 10 percent higher than the consumer price index on a 1972 base, but by 1983 the position had reversed. However, when we examine the prices of some individual food items, we find that two items, wheat (and bread) and rice, had declining real price trends while maize and sugar experienced rising trends.

Trends in real producer prices were estimated for four domestic crops—maize, wheat, rice, and sugar cane—and for four export crops—coffee, tea, pyrethrum, and seed cotton. However, while virtually all annual growth rates are insignificant, suggesting considerable fluctuations in real prices at some time during the period under review, for the period 1968–1980 most coefficient signs for annual growth rates are positive; for the longer period 1968–1983, virtually all are negative, indicating a decline in real producer prices in early 1980. In neither of the two periods, however, does there appear to be any marked difference in the behavior of food and export crop prices. Producer and consumer prices for rice and wheat show opposite trends.

Summarizing the information for Kenya presented in Chapter 6, the ratio of producer prices to world representative prices (for non-export crops) or to unit export value (for export crops) rose for all products except sugar cane and wheat (where it changed little) between 1968–1970 and 1978–1980. For export crops the ratios were particularly high and rose further, suggesting that the producers have been getting the world prices and that marketing costs have been well contained.

The foregoing analysis has assumed that the *actual* prices received by the producers are the same as official prices. In Kenya's case, because of the extremely high proportion of export crops and a significant proportion of the food crops handled by the marketing boards, it is reasonable to assume that the farm gate prices are likely to be close to the official producer prices. However, when there are significant surpluses or deficits in food production, the actual market prices may and do diverge from the official prices, but little information is available on this. Furthermore, for food crops grown by a large number of smallholders, such as maize, the official marketing channels may have a limited reach. In this connection, de Wilde has written: "The vast majority of smallholders are dependent on the illegal or unofficial market for both sales and purchases of maize and the prices in this market often depart widely from the official buying and selling prices."[4]

Impact of Public Policy on Prices

The trends in real producer prices result from an interaction among world prices, domestic inflation, and the exchange rate in addition to being influenced by the government criteria for price setting, commodity taxes, marketing board surpluses or deficits, and efficiency of the marketing system. For export crops, as already noted, the policy has been to relate domestic prices to world prices. Except for modest taxes on coffee during the commodity boom years 1976–1978, commodity taxes have not been levied to any significant extent. Nor have the marketing boards built up surpluses or accumulated deficits, except in recent years. On the other hand, there was a gradual increase in the overvaluation of the currency over the period 1968–1980. According to one measure, the overvaluation index increased by 43 percent between 1968–1970 and 1978–1980. This provides a rough estimate of the negative influence exerted by the exchange rate on producer prices. However, between 1980 and 1984 there was a significant devaluation of the Kenyan shilling, at least in relation to the U.S. dollar, from Sh.7.4 to Sh.14.4.

For food crops, the declared policy has been to relate the producer prices to world prices, but other considerations such as the impact on cost of living or incentives to producers have often played an important role in determining producer prices. As noted earlier, the ratio of domestic to world representative prices has tended to move up for all food items examined except sugar cane. This may in part be a consequence of the increase in the overvaluation of the currency. In the case of sugar, over this period Kenya moved towards self-sufficiency, which can be expected to depress the ratio.

The efficiency of the marketing arrangements has been the subject of extensive discussions and debates. While frequent allegations have been made about the shortcomings and inefficiencies of the agricultural marketing system, including widespread prevalence of bribery and corruption, relatively little information is available on the quantitative dimensions of the problem.[5]

• MALAWI •

The per head income in Malawi was estimated at $210 in 1982, which places it among the bottom quarter of the thirty-nine sub-Saharan countries for which relevant information is available. The per head GNP grew by 2.6 percent per year over the period 1960–1982, but with a marked slowdown since 1978. The country is heavily dependent upon agriculture, which accounted for 40 percent of GDP in 1982, down from 50 percent in 1960. The share of the manufacturing sector declined from 10 to 8 percent over the same period. Between 1960 and 1982 the proportion of the population in urban areas rose from 4 to 10 percent. In 1980 nearly 86 percent of the labor force drew its livelihood from agriculture. The two principal modes of agricultural production are small family farms and plantations, the latter accounting for over 60 percent of officially marketed output in recent years. The principal food crops are maize, cassava, paddy, and groundnuts, while to-bacco, tea, sugar, and cotton are export crops, as are groundnuts and rice. Estates specialize in tobacco, tea, and sugar.

Structure of Marketing and Pricing System

The estates and the smallholders are subject to different marketing and pric-ing systems. The bulk of the estate production of tobacco and tea is exported. The estates sell these crops through auctions in Malawi or elsewhere. There is thus no government regulation of marketing, and prices reflect world prices. Two-thirds of the estate sugar production is exported; the rest is sold domestically. The Government regulates both the wholesale and retail prices of sugar sold within the country.

The smallholders sell their products through local and village markets as well as through the state marketing agency, Agricultural Development and Marketing Corporation (ADMARC). ADMARC's domestic buying and selling prices are set in consultation with the government at the start of each season. According to ADMARC, the producer prices are fixed with the twin aim of ensuring a reasonable return to farmers while enabling ADMARC to earn a surplus to support national development programs. It fixes a uniform na-tional purchase and sales price for agricultural crops and inputs. Compul-sory procurement applies only to cotton, rice, and tobacco. In recent years a small number of growers of flue-cured tobacco (about 900) and of tea (about 3,700) have been able to sell their production at auctions through established organizations. In addition to buying from smallholders, ADMARC arranges for the sale of crops both domestically and abroad. It also supplies inputs to smallholders and has responsibility for agricultural de-velopment and agro-industrial enterprises. The smallholders can dispose of the surplus of the remaining crops through sales to other farmers, village and urban markets, or to ADMARC, which also acts as a residual buyer of crops such as maize, groundnuts, and cassava.

No significant changes have taken place in the marketing and pricing system in the 1970s. However, in February 1979, a price advisory committee was set up by the Government to review prices and alternative criteria for setting them. So far no report has been published by the committee.

Trends in Real Consumer and Producer Prices

The relevant price trends are summarized in Table 7.2. The relative price of food as measured by the cost of living index rose over the period 1969–1980

Table 7.2 Changes in Real Producer and Consumer Prices in Malawi

| | Producer Prices | | Consumer Prices | |
| | Annual Percentage Growth Rate | | | Annual Percentage Growth Rate |
Commodity	1968–80	1968–83	Commodity	1968–80
Seed Cotton	0.1 ns	–0.5 ns		
Tea	–0.4 [a] ns	–		
Tobacco	–5.1	–3.7		
Cassava	–4.7	–5.4	Cassava	0.6 ns
Groundnuts	1.8	1.8	Groundnuts	0.8 [b] ns
Maize	–1.5	–0.4 ns	Maize	3.2
Rice (Paddy)	–2.2	–4.6	Rice	9.6 [c]
Sugar Cane	–1.0 ns	–1.8	White Sugar	–0.8 [d] ns
			White Bread	–3.0 [d]

ns: not significant at the 10% level.
[a] 1968–79   [c] 1971–80
[b] 1968–78   [d] 1969–80
Sources: FAO data tapes, ILO *Yearbook of Labour Statistics*, Country Statistical Abstracts.

by 0.82 percent per year, which places the country in the middle of the group of seventeen countries for which this statistic was estimated (Table 2.7). Of the six food items examined, only the prices of sugar and bread fell, while there were marked increases for rice and maize. With respect to real producer prices, only groundnuts showed a statistically significant increase over the periods 1968–1980 or 1968–1983. Of the remaining seven commodities, price declines were particularly marked for tobacco, cassava, and paddy. In Malawi the distinction between domestic and export crops is less clear-cut than in most African countries. Only tobacco and tea may be described unambiguously as export crops, and maize and cassava as domestic crops although in recent years some maize has been exported to neighboring countries. Paddy, sugar, groundnuts, and seed cotton are both export and domestic crops. There does not appear to be any marked difference in the producer price behavior of domestic and export crops. It should also be noted that the producer and consumer prices show opposite trends for cassava, maize, and rice.

Summarizing the information for Malawi from Chapter 6, the ratio of producer prices to world representative prices (calculated for 1968–1970 and 1978–1980) declined for maize, paddy, and sugar while it rose for groundnuts. Producer prices as a proportion of unit export values fell for seed cotton and tobacco and rose for tea. In view of the different qualities of tobacco produced and different arrangements for smallholders and estates, it is difficult to interpret the available figures. However, as shown later, tobacco has been the one crop on which ADMARC has made the largest proportionate profits. The rate of profit on tobacco trading rose from 37 percent in 1972–1974 to 62 percent in 1976–1978. Thus, except for groundnuts and tea, which is an estate crop, there was a clear tendency for the producers to receive a declining proportion of the world prices in the 1970s.

To what extent can the official producer prices be taken as an accurate estimate of actual farm gate prices? As noted earlier, there is compulsory procurement for cotton, rice, and tobacco. Thus, for these commodities, the actual prices are likely to be close to official producer prices. For other crops—groundnuts, maize and cassava—ADMARC is a residual buyer but may still account for a significant proportion of marketed output. A survey in 1977 based on a year long collection of price data on fifteen selected commodities in 20 local markets indicated that the ADMARC prices on average tended to be lower than in the informal markets except in the more remote areas.[6]

Impact of Public Policy on Prices

Commodities are not subject to export taxes. The major direct influence on consumer and producer prices has been the fixing of consumer and producer prices by ADMARC in consultation with government; indirect influences include the exchange rate, the trading operations of ADMARC, and the efficiency of the marketing system.

Unlike the case in most African countries, the overvaluation index did not show any changes over the period 1968–1970 and 1978–1980. This implies that the exchange rate changes did not exercise any influence on changes in producer or consumer prices. In the subsequent period, 1980–1984, the local currency depreciated considerably against the U.S. dollar, going from 0.812 kwacha to 1.365.

The operations of ADMARC had the effect of considerably depressing the producer prices. Over a nine-year period in the 1970s, ADMARC realized trading profits of K.181.9 million, of which K.26 million was used to subsidize the consumption of staple foods (maize, rice, and general produce).[7] The net trading profits as a percentage of sales over the period 1972–1978 varied from 21.6 percent in 1973 to 38.5 percent in 1977, the average rising from 25.8 percent in 1972–1974 to 33.8 percent in 1976–1978. The average annual profit rates on sales in tobacco, cotton, and groundnuts over the period 1972–1978 were 49.2 percent, 23.5 percent and 24.9 percent, respectively. On the other hand, the operations on maize and rice yielded losses amounting to an annual average of 18.8 and 9.6 percent, respectively.[8]

The overall impact of public policies has been substantially to tax smallholder growers of export crops (tobacco, groundnuts, cotton) and to subsidize producers and consumers of food crops (maize and rice). While no recent estimates are available, for 1977 it was estimated that the ADMARC purchase price of maize was higher than the export parity price at local markets.[9] The effective subsidy to growers varied according to regions between 17 and 146 percent; the corresponding subsidy figures for rice farmers were 54 and 117 percent; and for groundnut growers effective taxation ranged from 116 to 150 percent. Presumably tobacco growers must have been subjected to taxation of similar orders of magnitude if not higher.

• ZAMBIA •

Income per head in Zambia was estimated at $640 in 1982, placing the country approximately in the top quarter of the sub-Saharan countries. The GNP per head has declined by 0.1 percent per year over the period 1960–1982. After a period of rapid growth in the first decade after independence, the economic situation has deteriorated massively since 1974. GDP per capita declined by 23 percent between 1974 and 1982, and real per head income fell even more sharply, by 44 percent. This is attributable largely to a drastic deterioration in the country's terms of trade.

Unlike the situation in most African countries, agriculture accounts for a relatively small proportion of total GDP: its share was 14 percent in 1982, having risen from 11 percent in 1960. The share of industry over the same period fell from 63 to 36 percent, while services rose from 26 to 50 percent. The initial relatively high share of industry and the subsequent sharp fall reflect the fluctuating importance of the mineral sector, especially copper. Despite the low share of agriculture in total GDP, 67 percent of the labor force was in this sector in 1980, having declined from 79 percent in 1960. On the other hand, nearly 45 percent of the population was estimated to be resident in urban areas in 1982, compared with 23 percent in 1960.

The main sources of agricultural production are about 800 large-scale commercial farmers, nearly 1,800 small-scale commercial farmers, and some 600,000 peasant farmers. The principal crops are maize, sorghum, millet, cassava, cotton, wheat, and tobacco. Of these tobacco and maize in some years are the only significant export crops. Sorghum, groundnuts, and cotton are exclusively or largely grown by small commercial and peasant farmers, while wheat is grown by large commercial farmers, with the marketed maize shared somewhat evenly between commercial and peasant farmers.

Structure of Marketing and Pricing System

Maize is the principal crop and also the major source of food in the country. The first attempt to control maize marketing was made in 1936 with the establishment of the Maize Control Board.[10] The Board was empowered to purchase and sell all maize at fixed prices in the areas served by rail. The prices were fixed to cover the cost of production and a reasonable return for the producers. Although in the early years the intention was to maintain prices above the world level, in actual practice beginning with 1940–1941, the producer and consumer prices were less than the import price. The predominant consideration was to keep food prices low in order to keep the cost of urban labor low. Often consumer prices were set below the producer prices and the marketing costs. This resulted in a subsidy from the government for the marketing board. These policies were continued up to and beyond independence. The coverage of commodities was extended to include at first groundnuts, and then beans, sorghum, and millet.

In 1964, the board changed its name to the Grain Marketing Board of Zambia (GMB). Its operations covered the line of rail and the Eastern Province and over time an increasing range of products such as cotton, oil seeds, fruits and vegetables, and fertilizers. Another board, the Agricultural Rural Marketing Board (ARMB) was set up in 1964 to operate in the more remote rural areas. The two boards were amalgamated in 1969 into the National Agricultural Marketing Board (NAMBOARD). In 1973, NAMBOARD was divested of its monopoly powers except for maize and cotton but continued to be residual buyer at fixed prices for other crops. In the Eastern, Northern, and parts of the Southern Province, the Board depends on the marketing cooperatives. There are also other parastatal boards for other crops. The principal ones are the Tobacco Board of Zambia, which apart from tobacco marketing is also concerned with provision of agricultural inputs and extension services; and the Lint Company of Zambia, which handles cotton.

The main features of the agricultural pricing and marketing system in Zambia in recent years can be summarized here. There is annual fixing of producer and consumer prices for most agricultural products by the Cabinet after consideration of the recommendations made by the Ministry of Agriculture and Water Development. The prices have been fixed at uniform levels throughout the country. The marketing of certain crops is carried out exclusively by the state marketing boards (NAMBOARD, Tobacco, Lint, etc.). For other crops, marketing boards act as residual buyers at fixed prices. In some areas marketing functions have been performed by cooperatives. Furthermore, the costs incurred by marketing boards and cooperatives (transport, handling, storage, and management) have been covered increasingly by government subsidies.

Different and conflicting criteria have been used in fixing prices. For tobacco, the criterion has apparently been to give the producers the auction prices. For maize and other staples, the prices are fixed on the basis of the following declared criteria: fair return to producers, fairness to consumers, cost of production, import-export parity, relative crop profitability, food security, and political acceptability. These criteria leave a wide margin for judgment.

Recently some significant changes have taken place in the marketing and pricing system, and others are likely to follow. In December 1982 the Government announced a decontrol of all wholesale and retail prices except for maize, wheat flour, bread, and fertilizers. Thus, although the marketing boards may continue to act as residual buyers at fixed prices, the producers, except for the products mentioned above, are free to sell to any buyer and at market prices. The functions of NAMBOARD were reduced to interprovincial trade of maize and fertilizers, the intraprovincial trade being handled by nine provincial cooperative unions. These measures were part of a larger package including devaluation and subsequently flexible exchange rates, sharp increases in producer and consumer prices, and reduction in subsidies to marketing boards and cooperatives.

Trends in Real Consumer and Producer Prices

The real price of food rose at an annual rate of 0.57 percent over the period 1970–1980, placing Zambia in the fifth lowest position out of seventeen countries for which this statistic has been computed (Table 2.7). For individual food items information was available only for maize and rice for the period 1974–1980, with the price of maize meal moving upwards while the price of rice fell sharply (Table 7.3). The real producer prices over the period 1968–1980 rose for wheat, maize, and seed cotton and fell for sugar cane and paddy. In recent years, there have been sharp increases in nominal and real producer prices for all commodities except for sunflower and seed cotton, as shown in Table 7.4. As shown in Chapter 6 the ratio of producer to world representative prices rose for maize, groundnuts, seed cotton, and

Table 7.3 Changes in Real Producer and Consumer Prices in Zambia

	Producer Prices			Consumer Prices
	Annual Percentage Growth Rate			Annual Percentage Growth Rate
Commodity	1968–80	1968–83	Commodity	1974–80[a]
Seed Cotton	4.1	0.6 ns		
Maize	1.0	1.4	Maize Meal	1.8 ns
Rice (Paddy)	−1.6 ns	−1.2 ns	Rice	−7.0
Sugar Cane	−3.1	−2.7[b]		
Wheat	4.9	4.1		

ns: not significant at the 10% level.
[a]The short period is dictated by absence of data for earlier years.
[b]1968–81

Source: FAO data tapes, ILO *Yearbook of Labour Statistics,* Country Statistical Abstracts.

Table 7.4 Increase in Agricultural Producer Price: 1974–84 (Percent)

Commodity	Nominal Terms	Real Terms
Maize	172	56
Wheat	112	21
Rice	150	43
Sorghum	200	71
Soya bean	110	20
Sunflower	57	−10
Groundnuts	103	16
Seed cotton	26	−28
Tobacco	85	6

Source: World Bank, *Zambia: Policy Options and Strategies for Agricultural Growth* (Washington, D.C.: World Bank, 1984).

wheat but fell sharply for sugar cane.

Impact of Public Policies on Prices

In Zambia the major influence on producer and consumer prices has been the direct fixing of prices by the government. The government has not resorted to commodity taxes for raising revenue. The exchange rate has been an important indirect influence in determining producer prices. Between 1968–1970 and 1978–1980, the overvaluation index moved up by about 13 percent, a relatively modest proportion as compared with most African countries. Between 1980 and 1984, the Zambian kwacha depreciated against the U.S. dollar from 0.79 to 1.75 kwacha. While the movement in overvaluation was modest, it can be argued that the level of exchange, influenced as it was by copper earnings, was relatively high and thus had a negative impact on producer prices. Certainly one consequence of the impact of the copper industry on wage levels and exchange rates was that Zambia never developed agricultural exports to any significant extent.

The level at which consumer and producer food prices have been set has, in fact, necessitated government subsidies to major agricultural parastatals. The subsidies increased from K.132 million in 1970–1973 to K.361 million in 1978–1982. The bulk of the subsidies, about 62 percent, went to cover the losses of one parastatal, NAMBOARD, which in effect constituted a fertilizer and maize subsidy. It is clear that if the government had not provided this subsidy, either the price to producers would have fallen or the consumers would have paid more or, more likely, both.

Apart from the losses incurred through the government pricing policy on inputs and produce, it has been argued that the costs have increased because of the growing inefficiencies of the marketing system.[11] The data cited in support of this contention concern the ratio of parastatal costs to f.o.b./ c.i.f. value of individual crops. The values of some of these ratios were 30 percent for wheat, 80 percent for soyabean, 51 percent for maize, 84 percent for sunflower, 85 percent for groundnuts, and 40 percent for seed cotton. Although the marketing inefficiencies may have increased, these figures do not in themselves provide any conclusive evidence.

Despite government subsidies to parastatals dealing with the marketing and processing of agricultural products, it has been argued that at least between 1965–1966 and 1974–1975 (the period for which calculations were made) most products received a negative nominal rate of protection (NRP).[12] Except for wheat and tobacco, all major agricultural products had a negative NRP; that is, the growers received less than the equivalent world prices. For most products this occurred in every year over the period. It has, however, been argued that the situation has changed dramatically since 1978 and that at present, as a result of a policy of high producer prices, most producers of agricultural commodities appear to be highly protected at the current foreign exchange rate.[13] Of the eleven commodities for which effective rates of protection (ERP) were estimated for 1980–1982, only virginia tobacco had negative rates. For others, the ERPs ranged from below 10 percent on burley tobacco to 2,233 percent on groundnuts. Furthermore, smallholders and emergent farmers had higher ERPs than either commercial farmers or state farmers, presumably a reflection of the smaller use of inputs by the former.

Summarizing the Zambian experience, it may be stated that the combination of the level at which producer prices were fixed and the high exchange rate caused by copper exports resulted in relatively low producer and consumer prices. Some of the effects of these policies were offset through subsidies to agricultural parastatals. In recent years the food prices and the real producer prices have increased sharply, and the latter appear to be above import parity prices for most commodities.

• NIGERIA •

With a per head income in 1982 of $860, Nigeria occupied the fifth highest position out of thirty-nine sub-Saharan African countries for which this information was assembled. The income per head grew at the relatively high rate of 3.3 percent per year over the period 1960–1982. The country experienced particularly rapid growth in the 1970s with sharp increases in the volume and price of petroleum exports. However, since 1980 there has been a drastic deterioration. Real GDP fell 12 percent in the 1981–1983 period, slipping a further 1 percent in 1984. Thus, per head income must have fallen by around 25 percent since the oil boom collapsed in 1980.[14]

Owing mainly to the discovery and exploitation of petroleum, the economy has undergone a major structural change since 1960. The relative importance of agriculture declined from 63 percent in 1960 to 22 percent in 1982, while that of industry rose from 11 to 39 percent over the same period. The share of services also rose from 26 to 39 percent. Despite this structural change, agriculture continued to be the main source of employment for the working population. The share of labor force in agriculture was 54 percent in 1980, having fallen from 71 percent in 1960. The proportion of population in urban areas rose from 13 to 21 percent between 1960 and 1982.

Despite the attempts in recent years to encourage plantations and large-scale farming, agricultural production is largely dominated by small, family farms. The importance of agricultural exports in absolute but more dramatically in relative terms declined sharply in the 1970s. The major export crops are cocoa, palm kernels, and rubber, while food crops comprise sorghum, millet, maize, groundnuts, rice, yams, and cassava. There is some specialization of production by region, with tubers and export crops cultivated in the south and cereals grown in the north.

Structure of Marketing and Pricing System

Nigeria has had a dual marketing and pricing system for most of the period. Under this system, the marketing and pricing of export crops was the responsibility of state marketing boards. On the other hand, the food and other domestic crops were largely left to private marketing and trading with little state interference. Although there have been some changes in this respect in recent years, essentially the system remains the same. The first marketing board was set up in 1948. Later it evolved into a series of marketing boards for such export commodities as cocoa, palm oil, palm kernels, groundnuts, and cotton. In 1955 the commodity marketing boards were converted into regional marketing institutions with responsibility for marketing all export crops within a particular region. In 1974 the federal government took over from the regional authorities the power to fix producer prices. In 1977 the regional marketing boards were dissolved and replaced by commodity boards—a reversion to the pre-1955 practice. Two of the seven marketing boards dealt with domestic products, the Nigerian Grain Board with guinea corn, maize, millet, wheat, rice, and beans and the Nigerian Tuber and Root Crops Board with yams and cassava. Other commodity boards established in 1977 were cocoa (dealing also with coffee and tea), groundnuts, cotton, palm produce, and rubber.

The export marketing boards have throughout the period been entrusted with the responsibility of fixing producer prices for growers of these products, purchasing crops from farmers through licensed purchase agents and selling them overseas through the Nigerian Produce Marketing Company. In contrast to marketing arrangements for domestic products, the marketing boards for export products are the sole legal authorities for purchase from the farmers through licensed traders. These purchases are made in principle at a single price throughout the country. Of course, in the late 1970s some of the products, such as cotton and groundnuts, have ceased to be export crops, and others have greatly declined in value; but the same system of price fixing and procurement continues for these products.

It is not possible to get accurate information on the criteria for establishing producer prices for export crops, but it appears that there have been significant changes over time in the criteria actually used. In the 1950s and 1960s, the marketing boards were used as a major instrument for accumulating surpluses from commodity sales. This policy was reversed in the 1970s. The sales and export tax levied on these products were also phased out in the 1970s. Thus, while in the 1960s the producer prices tended to be considerably below the world prices at the official exchange rate, for most products the situation was reversed in the late 1970s and early 1980s.

Until 1977 the food crops were not subject to regulation by state marketing boards. Although the two boards created in 1977 were entrusted with a wide range of responsibilities for food production, processing, and marketing, in actual practice they have played a negligible role in food procurement from the farmers. Likewise, the support prices established by the boards have been largely ineffective. The bulk of the food products continue to be traded through private channels and at prices determined by supply and demand. The marketing boards have exerted greater influence on food prices through the sale of imported food products. In addition, they have periodically purchased limited amounts of food for distribution at fixed consumer prices to selected institutions, mostly in urban areas.

Trends in Real Consumer and Producer Prices

The food price index rose less rapidly than the overall consumer price index till 1970, but in the subsequent period it tended to leap ahead. Thus in the 1970s in Nigeria, as in most other African countries, the relative price of food tended to increase. This trend was further accentuated between 1980 and 1984.

Table 7.5 clearly indicates the contrasting behavior of officially recorded real consumer and producer prices. Maize, yams, and to a lesser extent millet all rose while the real official producer prices of those items all fell. Indeed, the only clear exception is groundnuts, which experienced a rapid rise in producer prices. As shown below, there is considerable doubt as to whether these official prices reflect actual producer prices. The ratio of producer to world representative prices has tended to increase sharply for all four food crops for which it was possible to compute this information: groundnuts, soyabean, paddy, and maize (Chapter 6). The rapid decline in the quantity of export crops makes it difficult to provide comparable information for them.

To what extent did the official producer prices reflect the actual farm gate prices received by farmers? As indicated earlier, for export crops (or for what were export crops in the 1960s) such as cocoa, palm products, rubber, groundnuts, and cotton, the state marketing boards are the only or significant buyers of marketed output. Thus, it may be assumed that for these products the official prices approximate the actual prices received. On the other hand, for most food crops the official prices have only an indicative value. Given the fact that the real consumer prices for food have risen rapidly in Nigeria and that local food prices have increased more rapidly than imported food, as brought out in the official cost of living indices, it is somewhat surprising to find that except for groundnuts the real producer prices for all other food crops have tended either to decline or to remain basically unchanged, as for cassava and soyabeans. As the impact of state marketing operations on food prices is somewhat limited, we may be justified in concluding that the official producer prices give a misleading picture of the situation. It is highly likely that the real producer prices for most foodcrops have risen in the 1970s. This conclusion is also suggested by some other studies.[15]

Impact of Public Policy on Prices

The Nigerian experience can best be understood by dividing the period into

Table 7.5 Changes in Real Producer and Consumer Prices in Nigeria

Producer Prices		Consumer Prices	
Commodity	Annual Percentage Growth Rate 1968–80	Commodity	Annual Percentage Growth Rate 1968–80
Cassava	–0.44ns		
Groundnuts	8.6		
Maize	–4.6	Maize	7.7
Millet	–4.4	Millet	2.5 ns
Rice Paddy	–6.5	Rice	–0.8 ns
Sorghum	–2.7		
Soya Bean	0.7ns		
Yams	–5.9	Yams	4.6

ns: not significant at the 10% level.

Source: FAO data tapes, ILO *Yearbook of Labour Statistics*, Country Statistical Abstracts.

pre- and post-oil subperiods. In the 1950s and 1960s before oil became a significant export, the impact of public policy on agricultural prices was exerted primarily on export crops through state marketing boards and taxes. The returns to growers of export crops (cocoa, palm products, groundnuts, cotton, rubber) were reduced by export and sales taxes and surpluses accumulated by the marketing boards. The effective deduction rates for the five main crops varied from 20 percent for groundnuts to 42 percent for cocoa between 1947 and 1970.[16] There was also an increasing overvaluation of the local currency in the 1960s, thus exerting downward influence on producer prices. Several commentators have also remarked on the inefficiency and mismanagement of marketing boards, which have resulted in further reducing the returns to producers.

For food crops there was little direct intervention by the state but the real consumer and producer prices were of course affected by policies of import substitution and food imports. In the 1950s and early 1960s these factors were relatively insignificant, and thus the consumer and producer food prices may be considered to reflect largely the operation of free market forces. In the post-oil phase, the situation changed in a number of ways. First, the overvaluation of the currency tended to accelerate. Between 1968–1970 and 1978–1980, the overvaluation index rose by 80 percent. This in itself had a strongly depressive effect on prices of export commodities. This effect was counterbalanced by three factors. First, the export and sales taxes on export commodities were phased out by 1974. Secondly, instead of accumulating surpluses, the marketing boards became net recipients of subsidies. One indirect measure of this is the loans received by the commodity board from the Central Bank. These averaged N.365 million per year for the years 1979–1981, of which N.223 million was allocated to the Cocoa Marketing Board.[17] Finally, the government policy tended to fix producer prices at levels more attractive to growers. The impact of these policies can be seen in the rising ratio of producer prices to export unit value for most export crops in the 1970s and early 1980s.

The producer and consumer prices of food were affected more by trade policy and food imports than in the earlier period. Imports of wheat, rice, maize, and sugar rose rapidly, and the government pricing and distribution policy for imported food began to exert a stronger influence on food prices. The net import of cereals as a proportion of total supplies (imports plus domestic production) rose from 2.9 percent in 1967–1970 to 17.1 percent in 1979–1982. In the latter period, the dependency ratios for maize, rice, and wheat were 12.4, 32.5 and 98.0 percent, respectively.[18] Thus, particularly for rice and wheat, the import and distribution policy began to exert considerable influence on producer and consumer prices. But for other food crops government intervention in food pricing and marketing had only a limited impact, and the producer and consumer prices continued to be determined largely by the market forces.

As mentioned earlier, the ratio of producer to world representative prices rose for most food crops. Estimates made on the basis of the 1979 data concluded that all five products—paddy, maize, sorghum, millet, and groundnuts—enjoyed positive effective protection rates ranging from 50 percent for sorghum to 218 percent for paddy.[19] These values are reduced somewhat if we use a shadow price of foreign exchange of 79 percent of the official rate, but they still remain positive and ranged from 24 percent for sorghum to 166 percent for paddy.

To summarize the Nigerian experience, the consumer and most probably the producer food prices have risen in the 1970s. In the pre-petroleum era, the export crops were subjected to a series of deductions that substantially reduced the returns to growers. Agricultural exports have decreased in absolute and more sharply in relative terms in the 1970s. The increasing currency overvaluation has been a major contributory factor, but its effects have been partially offset by removal of taxes and replacement of marketing board surpluses by deficits. In the 1980s, the producer prices for most agricultural crops were considerably above the world prices at official rates of exchange.

• UNITED REPUBLIC OF TANZANIA •

With a per head income of $280 per year in 1982, the United Republic of Tanzania ranked fourteenth out of thirty-nine countries. With a growth in per head income of 1.9 percent per year over the period 1960–1982, the country can be classified among better performers in sub-Saharan Africa. However, in recent years the United Republic of Tanzania has encountered severe economic difficulties reflected in declining per head income, industrial excess capacity, and shortages of basic consumer goods. Agriculture is the most important sector of the economy, generating 52 percent of total output in 1982 as compared with 57 percent in 1960. The bulk of the population lives in rural areas, with 87 percent in 1982, having declined from 95 percent in 1960. Nearly 83 percent of the labor force derived their livelihood from agriculture in 1980, as compared with 89 percent in 1960.

The main forms of agricultural production are smallholders working on family, state, village communal, and large private farms. The main export crops are coffee, cotton, sisal, tobacco, cloves, pyrethrum, and cashew nuts, while food crops comprise maize, rice, wheat, sorghum, millet, cassava, and sugar. The smallholders are the main producers of coffee, cotton, cashew nuts, tobacco, pyrethrum, maize, drought staples, and to a lesser extent rice. State farms have important shares in the production of rice, wheat, sugar, and sisal while private estates account for significant production of tea and sisal. Village communal production is based largely on maize and, to a lesser extent, drought staples and cash crops.

Structure of Pricing and Marketing Systems[20]

In the years preceding and following independence the marketing of major crops, both food and export, was organized through marketing boards. The cooperative system played a part in collecting produce from the peasants, transferring it to areas where it was stored and marketed by the boards. This system continued until the mid-1970s, when the cooperatives were dissolved and their responsibilities transferred to a series of parastatal crop authorities.

The crops restricted to official marketing channels were the major domestic grains (maize, paddy, wheat), oilseed crops, cashew nuts, and cotton. All but the last of these were marketed through the National Agricultural Board. State intervention was directed at fixing the price at which marketing boards purchased scheduled crops from the regional cooperative unions. The price was fixed in advance of each crop season by the Economic Committee of the Cabinet after consultation with the appropriate technical department of the Ministry of Agriculture. Other marketing boards existed for cotton, tobacco, coffee, pyrethrum, sisal, and tea, but with the exception of cotton these crops were not subject to central government intervention in price determination. For most of them the prices paid by the boards to the cooperatives depended on their actual sales prices in export markets.

The change in the pricing and marketing system initiated in 1973 resulted in the replacement of the marketing boards by parastatal crop authorities with much wider responsibilities for production development and marketing of the crops under their control. Crop authorities were created for domestic food crops, oilseeds, cashew nuts, coffee, cotton, pyrethrum, sisal, sugar, tea, and tobacco. The marketing responsibilities of these ten organizations included, where applicable, the collection of crops from villages, transport, storage, further processing, and final sale either to domestic consumers or export markets. State intervention in agricultural pricing switched price fixing from the cooperative to the producer level, and geographical price variations at the producer level were eliminated. Thus, there was a single, pan-territorial producer price for each scheduled crop determined annually by the Economic Committee of the Cabinet. The Cabinet took decisions on the basis of the recommendation made by the Marketing Development Bureau of the Ministry of Agriculture. The price fixing was extended to include all export crops except coffee and sisal, whose price levels were determined on the basis of the price of sale actually realized after deduction of marketing costs and export taxes. In effect, the producer price was regarded as a residual to be obtained by deducting the estimated future cost of the parastatal from its estimated future sales realization.

In 1983 the government announced its intention to bring about significant changes in marketing and pricing policies.[21] These changes, which are to be introduced over a period of time, envisage the reestablishment of cooperatives and a reduced role for parastatal authorities. The cooperative unions will buy crops from the villages for resale to other institutions, including the marketing boards and crop authorities. For food crops, the village primary societies will be permitted to sell to adjacent societies or local retailers for local consumption and/or local processing. Similar arrangements will be allowed between adjacent cooperative unions. Long–range distribution for distant deficit areas and for major urban areas will be effected through the crop authorities and marketing boards. Crops for export will be purchased from the cooperative unions by crop authorities and marketing boards, but large commercial producers (both public and private) will be allowed to do their own marketing, including exporting. Where appropriate the sale of export crops will be organized through auctions in the United Republic of Tanzania.

As for pricing, the price differential system for different areas introduced in 1981–1982 will be continued and extended. Relative producer prices for different export crops will favor those that are high net foreign exchange earners. In fixing prices, "the rate of inflation as well as the costs of efficient production will be taken into account in order that as far as possible producers are assured of a reasonable return on their efforts, and that fairness prevails in the relative earnable income of rural and urban areas."[22]

Trends in Real Consumer and Producer Prices

The real price of food rose rapidly in the United Republic of Tanzania in the 1970s. Between 1969 and 1980, the annual increase of 1.71 percent was the second highest of the seventeen countries for which this statistic was computed (Table 2.7). When we examine the retail prices of three consumer food items over the period 1973–1980, we find that the price trend was positive for wheat and rice and negative for maize (Table 7.6). The real producer prices generally fell for export crops except coffee over the period 1968–1980 while they rose for most food crops with the exception of cassava. Over the period 1980–1984 prices generally declined for most export and food crops. As shown in Chapter 6, for most domestic crops the ratio of producer to world representative prices tended to increase between 1968–1970 and 1978–1980, while for export crops there was an opposite tendency. How-

Table 7.6 Changes in Real Producer and Consumer Prices in the United Republic of Tanzania

	Producer Prices		Consumer Prices	
	Annual Percentage Growth Rate			Annual Percentage Growth Rate
Commodity	1968–80	1968–83	Commodity	1968–80
Cashew Nuts	−3.3 ns	0.4 ns[1]		
Cassava	−2.7 ns	−6.6[4]		
Coffee	3.5 ns	0.3 ns[1]		
Cotton	−0.4 ns	−2.0		
Groundnuts	5.3	0.1 ns[2]		
Maize	4.5	1.9 ns[3]	Maize Meal (sembe)	−6.8[5]
Rice (Paddy)	1.0 na	0.4 ns[3]	Rice	1.5[5]
Sorghum	2.3	−0.8 ns[3]		
Sugar Cane	1.6 ns	−0.3 ns		
Tea	−3.6 ns	−6.0[1]		
Tobacco	−5.5	−5.7		
Wheat	0.2 ns	−1.7[3]	Wheat Flour	1.2 ns[5]

ns: not significant at the 10% level.
[1] 1971–83 [4] 1974–84
[2] 1971–84 [5] 1973–80
[3] 1968–84

Sources: FAO data tapes, ILO *Yearbook of Labour Statistics*, Country Statistical Abstracts.

ever, in the period since 1980 ratios for most products tended to move up owing to a fall in world prices.

To what extent are official consumer and producer prices a true reflection of the actual prices received or paid? For export crops, except for those living in the border regions, the possibilities of selling on the parallel markets are quite limited. On the other hand, for food crops there is considerable evidence, especially in recent years, of transactions in parallel markets for both consumers and producers. The evidence indicates that the average actual prices tend to be considerably in excess of the official consumer and producer prices, although the differential varies a good deal by region, season, and product. An indication of the magnitude of consumer price difference between official and parallel markets and of season and spatial differences is given in Table 7.7. The prices in March 1982 were 70 to 100 percent above those prevailing in September 1981, and the parallel market prices in Morogoro and Moshi were 100 to 150 percent higher than the official price in Dar. This differential became much greater in March 1982.

Another study based on the data collected over two years from informal village markets in thirteen villages in three lake regions likewise showed relative differentials between the official and informal market prices of between 1.5 and 5.0.[23] The average informal market prices were higher for all

Table 7.7 Parallel Market Prices for Rice In Selected Urban Centers (Sh./Kg.)

	September 1981	March 1982
Dar es Salaam	5.30 (official price)	--
Morogoro	10.30	17.40
Moshi	12.60	25.00

Source: Bureau of Statistics, cited in Marketing Development Board, *Price Policy Recommendations for the July 1982 Agriculture Price Review* (Dar es Salaam: Ministry of Agriculture, July 1982).

products—maize, rice, paddy, cassava, sorghum, and millet—but the differentials varied by crop and were greater in 1980–1981 than in 1979–1980. It may be concluded, therefore, that at least since the late 1970s the actual average consumer and producer prices for food crops have been higher than the official fixed prices.

Impact of Public Policy on Prices

The major influences on consumer and producer prices have been, apart from direct price fixing by the government, the movements of exchange rate, export taxes, the operation of the state marketing boards and food imports. Considering first the producer prices for export crops, the overall thrust of the public policy has been to reduce the prices below the levels that would have prevailed in the absence of state intervention. First, there was growing overvaluation of the currency in the 1970s. For instance, the overvaluation index increased by 44 percent between 1968–1970 and 1978–1980. The overvaluation increased further in the next two years, but the series of devaluations in 1983 and 1984 may have reversed the trend, as the value of the U.S. dollar rose from 9.28 to 15.12 shillings between 1982 and 1984.

The second major impact was due to export and sales taxes. These taxes, as a proportion of the total sales value of export crops, rose from 6.5 percent in 1970–1972 to 19.9 percent in 1978–1980. The major burden was borne by coffee, which in 1978–1980 accounted for 77 percent of the total export tax revenue, and the average rate of export taxes on coffee rose from 10.6 percent in 1970–1972 to 38.1 percent in 1978–1980.[24] In 1981 and 1982 most of these taxes were phased out except for minor levies on raw cashew nuts and pyrethrum.

The third major influence on producer prices for export crops was the operation of the commodity parastatals. Several commentators have argued that the growing inefficiencies of the parastatals dealing with crop marketing and processing have resulted in increased distribution costs and lower returns to growers of food and export crops. Ellis has shown that the share of producer value declined from 67.4 percent in 1970–1972 to 43.1 percent in 1978–1980 for export crops and from 45.6 percent to 38.2 percent for staple grains. The share of parastatal costs rose from 26.1 percent in 1970–1972 to 37.0 percent in 1978–1980 for export crops and for staple grains; the share of gross marketing margin increased from 55.0 percent to 61.8 percent over the same period. Ellis further argues that only a small part of the increase in the gross margin for export and food crops is represented by the new functions undertaken by the crop parastatals: ". . . a large proportion, and indeed the predominant proportion, of the increased resources committed to crop marketing were attributable to rapidly rising costs for the given set of core activities."[25] These rising costs are in turn attributed to three main factors: the creation of a large permanent bureaucracy consisting of managers, accountants, clerks, secretaries, etc.; the duplication of overhead capital between parastatals due to their specialization by crop rather than by geographical area; and the duplication of trained personnel and associated support facilities in agricultural research and extension.

The negative impact on producer prices of increasing overvaluation and growing marketing costs was partially offset by subsidies to parastatals. In the late 1970s and early 1980s there was a steady increase in the indebtedness of parastatals, financed by loans from the nationalized banking system. The annual interest charges (often the interest rates were below the market rates) as a proportion of 1981–1982 crop purchase value ranged from 2 percent for sugar to 29 percent for cotton and 95 percent for the National Milling Corporation, concerned with grains.[26] Ellis has estimated that for staple grain the implicit subsidy as represented by the deficits of the parastatals increased from nil in 1970–1972 to 29.6 percent in 1978–1980.

Thus, in summary, the producer prices for export crops were reduced in the 1970s by growing overvaluation of the currency, export taxes, and increasing marketing costs. The negative impact of these factors was partially offset by removal of export taxes, subsidies to parastatals, and (in 1983–1984) a more flexible exchange rate policy. For food crops, following the drought of 1973–1974 the government followed a policy of adjusting producer prices to maintain their value in real terms. The increasing marketing costs were offset by subsidies to parastatals. However, the growing reliance on food imports, both commercial and concessional, has enabled the government to hold in check the increases in consumer and producer food prices. The imports of food rose from nearly $3 million annual average in 1970–1972 to $38.3 million in 1978–1980. The net import of cereals as a percentage of total supplies increased from 2.7 percent in 1967–1970 to 13.7 percent in 1979–1982. The great bulk of these imports has been on concessional terms (79 percent in 1981).

Significant changes in policies affecting agricultural prices were initiated in the last two years. Under the measures taken in 1982–1983 as part of the Structural Adjustment Programme, there was devaluation of the shilling by 32 percent; nominal producer prices for export crops were raised by 40 percent and food crops by 30 percent; export taxes were abolished; restrictions were removed on interregional trade; and pan-territorial pricing for agricultural commodities was abolished. These reforms were carried further in June 1984. The shilling was devalued by another 40 percent from T.Sh.12.18 to T.Sh.17 to the U.S. dollar; producer prices were increased by 46–55 percent in nominal terms; and primary responsibility for crop procurement and delivery to marketing centers was restored to cooperatives.

• GHANA •

With a per head income of $360 in 1982, Ghana ranked almost exactly in the middle among thirty-nine sub-Saharan countries. Over the period 1960–1982, the GNP per head has declined at an annual rate of 1.3 percent, which puts Ghana among the four countries with the worst economic performance. There has been a steady worsening of performance from the early 1960s to the early 1980s. Most unusually, the share of agriculture in total output has risen from 41 to 51 percent between 1960 and 1982, while that of industry has fallen from 10 to 8 percent. The proportion of population in the urban areas has, however, risen from 23 to 37 percent over the same period. Nearly 53 percent of the labor force was in agriculture in 1980 as compared with 64 percent in 1960.

The bulk of agricultural production comes from family farms. Other forms of agricultural production are state farms and large private farms, but their contribution to agricultural output is relatively low. Cocoa is by far the most important export crop. Other export crops are coffee, rubber, fats and oils, and kola nuts. Main food crops comprise cassava, yams, plantain, maize, sorghum, millet, and paddy. There is some regional specialization of production, with tubers and cocoa grown in the south and cereals in the north.

Structure of Marketing and Pricing System

Export crops such as cocoa, coffee, cotton, and kenaf are subject to special marketing arrangements. The Cocoa Marketing Board was established in 1947, with responsibility for marketing, storage, handling, and export of cocoa. One of its important functions was to iron out annual price fluctuations and to secure greater stability in cocoa producer prices. Although its mandate was to fix cocoa producer prices on the basis of the world prices, over long periods of time the Board accumulated large surpluses that were diverted to other uses.

The food crops have generally been marketed through private channels. In the 1970s the government attempted to fix maximum retail consumer prices for a range of commodities. It also attempted to offer a minimum producer price for maize, rice, groundnuts, soyabeans, yam, sugar cane, plantain, cotton, and kenaf. Although in recent years the government has set up some parastatal marketing boards to purchase food crops from producers at fixed prices and to sell food at fixed consumer prices, in actual practice it has not been able effectively to control either the marketing or the producer or consumer price of these products. The Food Distribution Corporation (FDC) was set up in 1971 to deal originally with perishable crops but since 1975 also to market maize. The Rice Mills Unit was established as an autonomous unit in 1975 to implement the floor pricing policy of the government, buying paddy at a fixed price set by the government and selling milled rice at fixed prices wholesale. It did not, however, have monopoly rights of purchase or sales.

Trends in Real Consumer and Producer Prices

Ghana experienced the most rapid increase in real consumer food prices of the seventeen countries for which this information is available. The annual rate of increase was 2.51 percent over the period 1969–1980 (Table 2.7). Trends in real producer prices, as shown in Chapter 6, are dramatically different for export and food crops. The real producer prices of cocoa and coffee fell sharply over the period 1968–1980. On the other hand, most food crops experienced rising producer prices, especially marked for maize and plantain. These trends are also reflected in the ratio of producer price to world representative price or export unit values at official exchange rates. The ratio for cocoa and coffee fell significantly over the period 1968–1970 and 1978–1980, while it rose dramatically for maize, plantain, and paddy. For food crops these ratios rose in the late 1970s to multiples ranging between 4 and 9 (Chapter 6).

In the 1980s, an attempt was made partially to offset the price disincentives to export crops. The price of cocoa was raised from C2,743 per ton in 1978–1979 to C4,000 in 1979–1980, C12,000 in 1981–1982, C20,000 in 1983–1984, C30,000 in 1984–1985, and C56,600 in the 1985–1986 season. The producer prices for food crops were also raised, but their market prices are several times higher than controlled prices.

Impact of Public Policy on Prices

The overall thrust of public policy was massively to reduce the returns to growers of export crops, principally, of course, cocoa. This result was achieved through a combination of direct fixing of producer prices, export taxes and exchange rate policy. The producer prices were fixed at relatively low levels in relation to world prices. Furthermore, export and local duties were levied at relatively high rates.[27] Returns to producers were further reduced by the inefficiency and corruption of the Cocoa Marketing Board.

The impact on producer prices of export taxes and marketing costs is shown by the ratio of producer prices to export prices. This ratio fell from an average of 0.42 over the years 1969–1970 and 1971–1972 to 0.22 for the years 1976–1977 and 1978–1979. In the subsequent years there was a reversal of policy. The export taxes were phased out during 1981–1982 and were replaced by subsidies. The ratio rose to 0.85 in 1980–1981 and an average of 2.15 for 1981–1982 and 1982–1983.[28]

The third major influence on producer prices was the steady increase in the overvaluation of the currency that gathered momentum particularly after 1973. Between 1968–1970 and 1978–1980, the index of overvaluation rose by 240 percent, and it increased further in 1981 and 1982. However, in April 1983 the government instituted a number of key changes in exchange rate policy. It introduced a transitional system of multiple exchange rate resulting in de facto devaluation of 89 percent from a rate of C.2.75 per U.S. dollar to C.25. The rate applicable to cocoa and other traditional exports was C.23.38 to a dollar. A unified exchange rate system was introduced in October 1983, and the currency has been devalued several times since then with the rate in early 1986 being C90 to a dollar.

As for food crops, it was noted earlier that government efforts to control consumer and producer prices have been largely ineffective because of its limited share in the marketing of food crops. Food imports have risen fourfold over the past decade. The import dependency ratio for cereals rose from 16.5 percent in 1967–1970 to 23.2 percent in 1979–1982. In the latter period the ratios for maize, rice, and wheat were 9.4, 31.0, and 100 percent respectively. In 1981 the share of concessional food imports was 36 percent. The increasing dependence on cereal imports and the rising proportion of food aid in food imports has checked the rise in consumer and producer prices, but for other food crops the domestic market forces have substantially determined those prices.

In summarizing the Ghanaian experience, it may be stated that the prices for export crops were reduced drastically below the level that would have prevailed in the absence of state intervention. The main instruments were direct price fixing, export taxes, and overvalued exchange rate. There was a reversal of policy in all these respects in the 1980s, which resulted in a reduction of the discrimination suffered by cocoa growers. In the food sector government efforts to control prices were largely unsuccessful and prices continued to be influenced mainly by market forces. For wheat and rise, imports exerted a major influence on prices.

• SUMMARY •

In this section we draw upon the preceding discussion of country experiences in agricultural marketing and pricing to highlight similarities and divergences in structures and policies. A common pattern observed in all countries is the extensive and increasing involvement of the state in agricultural marketing and pricing through most of the period. As shown later, it is only since 1982 or 1983 that there has been some reversal of this trend. However, the objectives and scope of state intervention have varied by country and often over time.

In Kenya and Zambia the marketing boards were first created to provide protection for European agriculture and covered the staple foods in the first instance. While in Kenya the protectionist stand continued to dominate policy, in Zambia the predominance of mining interests soon shifted the concern of the government towards keeping low the price of basic foodstuffs. In Nigeria and Ghana, on the other hand, the marketing boards were created to siphon off surplus from the sale of export crops. In Malawi, the marketing board has effectively served as an instrument of surplus extraction from the peasant production of export crops and of subsidy of food crops. Finally, in the United Republic of Tanzania, state intervention and controls came as an essential part of a policy of an increasingly centrally planned economy and served also to extract surplus from peasant production. In eastern and southern African countries the government policy did not make any distinction between food and export crops. The state role in pricing and marketing extended to all crops and, except for Malawi, did not distinguish between large and small farmers. In Ghana and Nigeria, despite recent attempts by the governments to extend state control over food crops, the policy has focused largely on export commodities.

All countries experienced a rise in the relative consumer price of food. But there was a great deal of variation with respect to real producer prices. In Kenya, producer prices for the majority of both export and food crops tended to move up while, interestingly enough and contrary to what is generally believed, they tended to decline in Malawi. In Ghana and the United Republic of Tanzania, the real producer prices of the majority of food and export crops show opposite trends, the former rising and the latter falling. In Nigeria also this is the most probable scenario. It is difficult to classify Zambia along these lines as there are no major export crops. The real producer prices tended to decline for most of the important crops such as maize, tobacco, sugar cane, and paddy but rose for a few crops such as wheat and seed cotton.

The countries also display considerable diversity with respect to the mechanisms used to influence producer and consumer prices. While they all used direct price fixing with varying degrees of success to determine agricultural prices, the influence of other mechanisms varied. Increasing overvaluation of the currency was a factor in all countries, but its incidence was greatest in Ghana and Nigeria and lowest in Zambia and Malawi. Commodity taxes were important in Nigeria and Ghana but were phased out in the 1970s in the former. In the United Republic of Tanzania also they became important in the late 1960s and 1970s. Kenya, Zambia, and Malawi did not use commodity taxes to any significant extent. Nigeria and Ghana used surpluses by the marketing boards to extract additional resources from the agricultural sector. Malawi also resorted to this device to tax peasant agriculture. On the other hand, Kenya, Zambia and the United Republic of Tanzania did not make use of this device to squeeze agriculture. Finally, the increasing inefficiencies and mismanagement of marketing boards appear to have been a common factor in all countries, albeit in varying degrees, in depressing producer prices.

The global recession and the growing agricultural crisis in Africa have led to significant changes in marketing and pricing policies in the 1980s. The governments have been attempting to provide more attractive producer policies for agricultural crops but in some cases these efforts have been frustrated by falling export prices and galloping domestic inflations. Many countries have tended to place greater reliance on exchange rate flexibility as a policy instrument. Export taxes have been phased out in the United Republic of Tanzania and Ghana. In several countries—the United Republic of Tanzania, Ghana, Nigeria and Zambia—the marketing boards have been incurring losses in recent years and receiving government subsidies. Finally, in most countries significant changes are being introduced in the marketing system designed to enhance efficiency by increasing the role of private traders and cooperatives and reducing the monopoly exercised by state marketing boards.

• NOTES •

1. All these figures, unless otherwise stated, are taken from the World Bank publications, especially *Toward Sustained Development in Sub-Saharan Africa* (Washington, D.C., 1984).

2. For an account of the origin and development of the agricultural marketing system in Kenya, see Judith Heyer, "The Marketing System," in J. Heyer, J. K. Maitha

and W. M. Senga, eds., *Agricultural Development in Kenya* (Nairobi: Oxford University Press, 1976).

3. John C. de Wilde, *Agriculture, Marketing, and Pricing in Sub-Saharan Africa* (Los Angeles: University of California, 1984).

4. Ibid., p. 17.

5. See G. Schmidt. "Effectiveness of Maize Marketing Controls in Kenya," in J. T. Mukui, ed., *Price and Marketing Controls in Kenya,* Institute of Development Studies Occasional Paper No. 32 (University of Nairobi, 1979).

6. World Bank, *Malawi: Growth and Structural Change: A Basic Economic Report* (Washington, D.C., 1982).

7. J. Kydd and R. Christiansen, "Structural Change in Malawi Since Independence," *World Development* (May 1982).

8. World Bank, *Malawi: Growth and Structural Change.*

9. See World Bank, *Malawi: The Development of the Agricultural Sector* (Washington, D.C., 1981).

10. For more details on the evolution of the marketing system, see Doris Jansen Dodge, *Agricultural Policy and Performance in Zambia* (Berkeley: University of California, 1977); and World Bank, *Zambia: Policy Options and Strategies for Agricultural Growth* (Washington, D.C., 1984).

11. World Bank, *Zambia: Policy Options and Strategies.*

12. Doris Jansen Dodge, *Agricultural Policy and Performance.* NRP is estimated by comparing producer prices with import parity prices, after taking into account fertilizer subsidy.

13. World Bank, *Zambia: Policy Options and Strategies.*

14. *Financial Times,* 8 January 1985.

15. See Paul Collier, "Oil and Inequality in Rural Nigeria," in Dharam Ghai and Samir Radwan, eds., *Agrarian Policies and Rural Poverty in Africa* (Geneva: ILO, 1983).

16. P. Clough and G. Williams, "Marketing With and Without Marketing Boards: Cocoa, Cotton and Grain Marketing in Nigeria" (unpublished, 1982).

17. Central Bank of Nigeria, *Annual Report and Statement of Accounts,* 1981.

18. FAO/UNDP, *Assistance to the National Grains Production Company Limited,* Interim Report on Nigeria (Rome: FAO, 1984).

19. World Bank, *Nigeria: Macro-economic Policies for Structural Change* (Washington, D.C., 1983).

20. This account draws heavily on F. Ellis, "Agricultural Price Policy in Tanzania," *World Development* 10, no. 4 (1982).

21. The broad outline of the policy changes is given in *The Agricultural Policy of Tanzania* (Dar es Salaam: Ministry of Agriculture, 1983).

22. Ibid.

23. Reported in Andrew G. Keeler et al., "The Consumption Effects of Agricultural Policies in Tanzania" (unpublished, Sigma One Corporation, 1982).

24. F. Ellis, "Agricultural Marketing and Peasant-State Transfers in Tanzania," *Journal of Peasant Studies* 10, no. 4 (July 1983).

25. Ibid.

26. Marketing Development Board, *Price Policy Recommendations for the July*

1982 Agriculture Price Review (Dar es Salaam: Ministry of Agriculture, July 1982).

27. Assefa Bequele, "Stagnation and Inequality in Ghana," in Dharam Ghai and Samir Radwan, eds., *Agrarian Policies and Rural Poverty.*

28. World Bank, *Ghana: Policies and Program for Adjustment,* vol. 2 (Washington, D.C., 1983).

·8·

Equity Impact of
Agricultural Prices

The foregoing chapters have focused on changes in real agricultural prices in sub-Saharan African countries and have examined the price trends and policies in somewhat more detail in six countries. The purpose of this chapter is to analyze the equity implications of agricultural price trends. By way of providing background information, the first section gives a broad picture of rural income distribution and of the processes sustaining differentiation in sub-Saharan Africa. This is followed by a discussion of the framework for analyzing equity impact. This framework is then used to trace, within the limits of the data available, some of the main equity effects of the pattern of agricultural price changes in African countries in the 1970s. These effects are illustrated through a somewhat more detailed analysis of the equity impact of agricultural price trends in four selected countries: Kenya, the United Republic of Tanzania, Zambia, and Malawi.

• INCOME DISTRIBUTION AND DIFFERENTIATION
IN RURAL AREAS •

Much of sub-Saharan Africa is mercifully free from many of the iniquitous institutions and processes that are characteristic of the agrarian systems of many countries in Asia and Latin America, such as massive landlessness, extensive peasant indebtedness to money-lenders and harsh tenancy and sharecropping arrangements.[1] But rural differentiation has advanced further in sub-Saharan Africa than is generally recognized, and the problems of malnutrition and hunger continue to be severe and persistent.

The evidence on income and land distribution in Africa has been reviewed elsewhere.[2] Despite their well-known limitations, the available data point to certain conclusions. The estimated gini coefficients of rural income distribution vary between 0.30 and 0.40 for the United Republic of Tanzania, Lesotho, Sierra Leone, Zambia, and Sudan, where a relatively low coefficient indicates relatively equal income distribution. These figures are comparable to those for many Asian countries. Rural inequalities in Kenya and Botswana, as illustrated by ginis of 0.50, appear high by international standards. While no comparable figures are available for other countries, some evidence indicates that in those in which commercial agriculture has penetrated more deeply, such as Senegal, Ghana, Côte–d'Ivoire, and Nigeria, the indices of inequality would be higher than those for the first group. In Ghana, for instance, overall figures for the rural sector are not available, but among the cocoa growers, who in 1970 formed about 22 percent of the rural labor force, the share in total income of the bottom 20 percent was 5 percent compared with 50 percent for the highest 20 percent. In Nigeria, on the basis of many village studies over different periods, the income differential between the top 10 and the bottom 10 percent of cocoa growers ranged from 7 to 1 to 20 to 1. For food producers, the differentials were on the order of 4 to 1.

Some indirect evidence on rural income inequalities is provided by estimates of gini coefficients for land distribution in a number of African countries. The inequalities appear to be substantially greater than might be deduced from the popular notions of land abundance, customary land tenure system, and family-based subsistence cultivation. They support the estimates of comparatively large income inequalities presented earlier. On the whole, the estimates of gini coefficient of land concentration appear to be well below those of Latin America, but roughly similar to those of Asia. The majority of the African countries have land concentration ratios between 0.37 and 0.48, which makes them comparable to Sri Lanka, the Republic of Korea, and Thailand. The higher figures for Kenya, Botswana, and Ghana (between 0.50 and 0.64) are nearer to those found in the Philippines, Pakistan, Bangladesh, and India.

Data are even less satisfactory for analyzing changes in income distribution. The patterns and processes of rural change in most African countries strongly suggest a trend towards a worsening of income distribution. Limited evidence from individual countries points in the same direction. In the Central and Nyanza provinces of Kenya, which have 76 percent of all smallholders, the share in both income and land of the bottom 40 percent declined from 1963 to 1974. In Ghana the share of cocoa earnings of the bottom 40 percent of growers declined from 1964 to 1970 while that of the top 10 percent rose sharply. In Nigeria, village studies in food–producing areas suggest that the land share of the bottom 40 percent has been declining while that of the top 10 percent has been increasing. There is also evidence of increasing concentration of cattle ownership in pastoral economies such as Botswana and Somalia. The emergence of "progressive" farmers accounting for a significant proportion of cash crops in Zambia, Côte–d'Ivoire, and Malawi suggest a rising share in rural incomes received by the top 10 to 20 percent of smallholders.

The figures on agricultural growth in the 1970s and early 1980s imply falling production per rural inhabitant in at least twenty-five African countries. Farmers' incomes have been further eroded by a variety of government policies. Thus, the great majority of the rural population in these countries suffered declines in real incomes in the 1970s. Where income distribution has also deteriorated, the decline in the incomes of the poorer sections must have been very severe indeed. These groups comprise predominantly subsistence farmers, peasants and nomads living in marginal and disadvantaged areas, agricultural employees, and households headed by women.

An increasing proportion of the population has benefited from social services such as health and education. An index of the improvement in health services is the rise in life expectancy at birth from 39 to 47 years from 1960 to 1979 and the decline in the child death rate from 38 to 25 per 1,000. Likewise, the adult literacy rate is estimated to have jumped from 16 to 28 percent over 1960–1976 and enrollments in primary schools rose from 36 to 63 percent of that age group between 1960 and 1978. However, it is not known to what extent the rural population, particularly the disadvantaged, has benefited from expansion in social services. Furthermore, many of these advances are now threatened by the economic crisis.

The roots of growth in rural inequalities go back to the early colonial days when policies of land alienation for foreign settlers and companies, encouragement of cash crop production by peasant farmers, and concentration of public expenditures in better endowed areas combined to intensify existing inequalities. Some of these policies were continued after independence. The cultivation of export crops was generally the first step. Those who had land in the "right" areas and were selected as "progressive" farmers had significant increases in incomes. This provided the savings for further investment in land and expansion or diversification of production.[3] In many cases, trading or other non-farming activities provided the surplus for land acquisition.[4] Earnings from jobs in the urban areas have in some cases been important sources of funds for purchase of land and livestock.[5] State policies have greatly accelerated growth in rural inequalities. Extension services, supply of credit, seeds, fertilizers, tools, and other inputs have generally been concentrated on the more developed areas and the better-off farmers. In most countries the political, bureaucratic, and business elites have used the machinery of state to acquire farms or participate in subsidized agricultural development schemes.

These are some of the mechanisms that have led to the emergence of a class of relatively prosperous farmers variously called progressive, commercial, or emergent. Some of the largest are urban-based absentee farmers. At the other end of the scale, a rapidly increasing number of households confront pressures forcing down their meager living standards. Land scarcity has been a problem in Kenya, Malawi, Rwanda, Burundi, Zimbabwe,

Lesotho, Swaziland, Mauritania, Niger, southeastern Nigeria, the western highlands of Cameroon, the Mossi plateau of Burkina Faso, and Senegal's northern Groundnut Basin. Pressure of population, often combined with inequalities in land distribution, is leading to landlessness in some areas. Because of excessively small holdings some members of the household are forced to earn income through casual employment. The scarcity of land further contributes to reduced yields and lower incomes through soil deterioration. It has also led to migration to more arid zones where, as in Kenya, incomes are lower and more uncertain. For households on the margin of subsistence with small cash incomes, a family misfortune or a drought can lead to irreversible loss of land or livestock.[6] Rapid inflation, stagnant cash incomes, and inflexible expenditure items have driven many into debt, sale of assets, and penury. Although the majority of peasant households, particularly in less advantaged areas, have been largely bypassed by government programs for agricultural development, they have not escaped taxation and inflation.

In general, the processes of differentiation have gone farthest in countries that have had a relatively long period of commercial agriculture and more freedom for market forces and private investment, or where the earlier pattern of land alienation and settlement had created strong racial inequalities. Differentiation is more limited in countries at an earlier stage of development with greater preponderance of subsistence production and less disruption of the traditional system of land use and agricultural production. During the period under review a number of countries, including the United Republic of Tanzania, Mozambique, Angola, and Ethiopia, have attempted to achieve rural development through different institutional means with the common objective of controlling polarization of incomes and wealth. With the exception of the United Republic of Tanzania, which has contained rural differentiation, either the experience has been too recent or too little is known for a useful assessment.

• FRAMEWORK FOR EQUITY ANALYSIS OF AGRICULTURAL PRICE CHANGES •

Changes in any price potentially affect both the real incomes of consumers and users of the commodity concerned as well as the incomes of the factors involved in the production of the commodity. In addition to the direct effect on the incomes of users and producers, the price changes are likely also to generate secondary, indirect effects. These effects arise from substitution in consumption induced by initial price changes as well as from changes in production caused by adjustments in scale and techniques of production.[7] The indirect effects may attenuate price changes or, depending upon the time period, may in some cases reverse the direction of initial price changes. Thus, the full effects of price changes can only be captured in a dynamic, general equilibrium analysis. Unfortunately, such analysis is difficult and, given the data limitations in most African economies, is in any case not possible or justified. We have, therefore, attempted to devise an alternative framework that, while theoretically inferior, will nevertheless capture the most significant equity effects of price changes. The emphasis is on direct equity impact though at times reference is also made to possible indirect effects. In order to ease the analysis, we first consider the impact on consumers of food price changes reserving for later the impact on producers.

Changes in food prices affect all individuals and households since food is consumed by all. The effect on the real incomes of the poor is especially great as they spend a substantially greater proportion of their income on food. The key features determining the equity impact of, say, a rise in food prices in a country, appear to be the level of per head income; the degree of inequality in income distribution in rural and urban areas, and thus the size and location of poverty groups; and the size of the working class, i.e., those whose primary source of income is wage employment and who are thus dependent on purchases to meet their food needs. Other things being equal, the higher the increase in food prices, the lower the per head income, the greater the concentration in income distribution, the larger the relative size of the working class, and the lower the increase in money wages of low-income workers, the more serious the adverse effects on welfare.

Apart from these general factors, the actual welfare effects of changes in food prices are likely to be influenced by the specifics of the marketing and food distribution system in each country. In this context, the issue of access to food is particularly important. In a situation of scarcity of food and poor marketing and transportation systems, residents living outside the main centers and relying on food purchases from the center may have inadequate or no access to food. Likewise, in a situation where the government attempts to sell food at fixed prices, unless it has substantial control over food marketing it is all too likely that only privileged consumers and residents in major cities will be in a position to purchase their requirements at official prices. Most other consumers may have to pay the higher prices prevailing in the parallel markets. Thus, in order to determine the welfare impact of food price policies, one would need to have information on the access to food of people in different parts of the country and actual food prices in different markets.

In turning now to the impact on producers of agricultural price changes, it is necessary to take into account both food and export crops. The equity impact will be determined by, among other things, disparities in distribution of assets and income among as well as between the rural and urban households, change in agricultural prices, and the pattern of agricultural output by income or land size. Other things being equal, the welfare effects of producer price increases will be less favorable the greater the disparity in assets and incomes, for in this situation the bulk of the benefits will flow to the better-off farmers who provide most of the marketable surplus. To the extent the small farmers benefit from improvement in producer prices, this should lead to an overall improvement in income distribution in situations where their average incomes are lower than those of the urban working class. The pattern of agricultural price changes and of output by income category has equity effects insofar as there is a differential change in producer prices of different crops and there are differences in the pattern of crop cultivation by income groups.

Apart from the direct impact on producer incomes of changes in agricultural prices, the indirect effect through changes in production and employment over time is likely to be more important on the production than on the consumption side. Unfortunately, it has not been possible to capture this in the following analysis, which thus concentrates largely on the direct equity impact of price changes.

• EQUITY IMPACT OF CHANGES IN CONSUMER FOOD PRICES •

An increase in the real consumer food price in practically all African countries was perhaps the most significant agricultural price change in the 1970s (Table 2.7). Since food is a major item of expenditure for the poor, rapid increase in relative food prices in most African countries would have had a serious adverse effect on their real incomes and welfare unless offset by a rise in wages and other sources of income. The poor in African countries may be divided into at least four distinct categories: unskilled, low wage employees in urban areas; workers in the urban informal sector; agricultural employees; and subsistence and poor peasants who grow food for family consumption and may have recourse to other sources of income—part-time seasonal employment, remittances, sale of beer, etc.—to meet cash needs for taxes, school fees, and basic consumer goods including food. In several countries where internal or external migration is an important phenomenon, as in southern African and Sahelian countries, female-headed households are likely to constitute a significant proportion of the last-mentioned group.

The poor are likely to suffer most from the rising food prices, first because their incomes are low and secondly because a high proportion of their total income is spent on food. Household expenditure surveys in urban areas in Africa indicate that urban dwellers on average devote 30 to 50 percent of consumer expenditure to food and drinks with wage–earners spending even more, perhaps 50 to 60 percent. The rural households spend larger proportions of their total income (including subsistence income) on food because of their generally lower average incomes and lower expenditure on rent and transport. The poorer households in both rural and urban areas spend proportionately more on food and drinks.

In analyzing the equity impact of a rise in real consumer food prices, we employ the framework outlined earlier. The results of this analysis for eleven countries are summarized in Table 8.1. The final column of the table is our own subjective ranking of the likely impact on equity of the changes in consumer food prices experienced in the 1970s. This incorporates our own implicit weighting of the relative importance of the factors considered in the other columns; in any formal analysis these weightings would have to be made explicit.

It will be noted that in Zimbabwe and Mauritius the relative price of food declined. The beneficial effects of such a development are reinforced by the fact that both these countries have a high degree of proletarianization, and the real wages of workers, in both agriculture and non-agriculture, rose over the period 1972–1979, with non-agricultural wages rising more rapidly in Mauritius and agricultural wages in Zimbabwe. Of course, the high degree of income and asset concentration in Zimbabwe, in both rural and urban areas, implies that despite the middle–income status of the country, the bulk of the population in the country must have had relatively low income levels. The sharp concentration of assets and incomes in that country offsets to some extent the otherwise favorable effects of price changes.

At the other extreme, the relative food prices rose rapidly in Ghana, the United Republic of Tanzania, and Nigeria, and to a somewhat lesser extent in Sierra Leone. In Nigeria, the degree of proletarianization is moderate and the effects of higher food prices were more than offset by rises in money wages for both agricultural and non-agricultural employees. This is a reflection to some extent of the extremely rapid growth of the economy in the 1970s. At the same time, the polarization in rural areas appears to be relatively modest. It may thus be argued that the adverse effects of a rapid rise in relative food prices were probably quite limited, confined possibly to small groups in urban and rural areas unable to increase their money incomes.

In the other three countries in this category—Ghana, the United Republic of Tanzania, and Sierra Leone—the rise in food prices was reflected in declining real wages for agricultural and non-agricultural employees, the decline being particularly severe for Ghana and Sierra Leone. The quantitative dimensions of this were somewhat moderated by the low degree of proletarianization of the United Republic of Tanzania and Sierra Leone although the lower per head incomes in these countries must have resulted in relatively greater hardships for those adversely affected in both urban and rural areas. In many respects the outcome in Ghana appears to have been the worst. The relative rise in food prices was the highest in Africa. The degree

Table 8.1 Equity Effects of Rise in Food Prices

Country	Rise in Relative Food Price[1]	Per Head Income[2]	Urbanization[3]	Proletarianization[4] Overall	Proletarianization[4] Rural	Real[5] Urban Wages	Real[5] Rural Wages	Differentiation Overall	Differentiation Rural[6]	Equity Impact[7]
Ghana	H	M	H	H	H	–	–	H	H	– –
Côte-d'Ivoire	M	H	H	M	M	–	–	H	H	–
Kenya	L	M	L	M	M	–	+	H	M	+
Malawi	M	L	L	M	H	+	–			–
Mauritius	N	H	H	H	H	+	+			+++
Nigeria	H	H	M	M	L	–	+	H	M	+
Sierra Leone	H	L	M	H[4]	L	+	–	H	M	– –
Swaziland	L	H	L	H	H		+			++
United Republic of Tanzania	H	L	L	L	L	–	–	M	L	–
Zambia	M	M	H	M	L	–	–	H	M	–
Zimbabwe	N	M	H	H	H	+	+	H	H	++

N = Negative; L = Low; M = Medium; H = High

[1] H is more than 1.2 percent per year; M is between 0.60–1.2 percent per year; L is less than 0.60 percent per year; N is decline.

[2] H is more than $500.00 per year; M is between $300.00 to $500.00 per year; L is less than $300.00 per year.

[3] H is more than 30 percent; M is between 15 to 30 percent; L is less than 15 percent.

[4] Overall: H is more than 20 percent of labor force; M is between 10 to 20 percent of labor force; L is less than 10 percent of labor force.

[5] Between 1972 and 1979 for all countries except for Tanzania and Zambia where it is up to 1978.

[6] Based on estimates made in Dharam Ghai and Samir Radwan, eds., Agrarian Policies and Rural Poverty in Africa (Geneva: ILO, 1983); S. Jain, Size Distribution of Income: A Compilation of Data (Washington, D.C.: World Bank, 1975); and ILO/JASPA, Rural-Urban Gap and Income Distribution: A Comparative Sub-Regional Study (Addis Ababa: ILO/JASPA, 1983).

[7] Ranking most favorable+++; least favorable – – –. The ranking is highly tentative and preliminary, and based of course only on the impact on consumers.

of proletarianization, including that in rural areas, is quite high, and employees in both agriculture and non-agriculture appear to have suffered significant declines in real wages. Furthermore, the country is characterized by a high degree of rural differentiation.

Malawi, Côte–d'Ivoire, and Zambia are among countries that experienced moderate increases in relative food prices. All three countries are characterized by a moderate degree of proletarianization, the emphasis in Zambia being on non-agricultural employment with farming employment quite significant in the other two countries. Furthermore, the real wages of employees fell in Zambia and Malawi and most likely in Côte–d'Ivoire, particularly in agriculture. It is interesting that in Malawi and Côte–d'Ivoire the real wages fell despite an extremely rapid growth of the economy and of wage employment including the agricultural sector. In Malawi the fall in real wages is a reflection of the tough wages policy pursued by the government, and in Côte–d'Ivoire it has resulted in part from the unlimited supply of labor generated by migration from the north and from the neighboring countries.

Swaziland and Kenya have experienced low increases in the relative price of food. The former is a relatively high–income country with significant proletarianization. It appears that real wages in both agriculture and non-agriculture have risen extremely rapidly, and thus the adverse effects of increases in food prices must have been confined to groups of urban unemployed and of poorer rural households that are net food purchasers. Kenya is characterized by a moderate degree of proletarianization but considerable rural differentiation. While the real wages of agricultural employees rose between 1972 and 1979, there was a substantial fall in those of non-agricultural employees.

• EQUITY IMPACT OF CHANGES IN REAL PRODUCER PRICES •

In order fully to analyze the equity implications of relative price changes, it would be necessary to construct the barter and income terms of trade for agricultural producers. It has not been possible to do this here although in the country experiences discussed in the next section the available information on the farmer terms of trade is summarized. Here we attempt to sketch some likely effects on equity of trends in real prices of selected agricultural products noted in Chapter 6. It should be noted that this can give only a partial picture of the equity implications for farmers of changes in relative prices. The discussion of real producer prices of agricultural products in Chapter 6 brought out the diversity of experience by country and by crops within individual countries. Any simple generalizations are thus likely to be misleading. To the extent that one can make any generalizations at all about the trends in real producer prices in the 1970s, it appears that for the majority of countries and crops the real producer food prices showed a positive trend, while the opposite was true for cash crops. This trend seems to have become even more evident in the 1980s.

What are the broad equity implications of such a pattern of agricultural price trends? Ignoring for the moment all the necessary qualifications in terms of specific crops, relative price changes, country specificities about structure of income distribution, and pattern of agricultural production, one can hazard three general points. First, the total marketed value of export crops is severalfold the value of marketed domestic crops. Thus, the overall impact on incomes of agricultural producers of the pattern of price changes observed in the 1970s and early 1980s is likely to be negative. Other things being equal, the price changes would reinforce rural-urban income inequalities. But what about intrarural inequalities?

This brings us to the second point, which is that there is no automatic correlation between export crops and large farms. While plantations continue to be associated in many countries with export crops, such as in Malawi, Swaziland, Mauritius, Zaire, and Côte–d'Ivoire, there is no such correlation in other countries with a significant large farm/estate sector, such as Kenya, the United Republic of Tanzania, Zambia and Zimbabwe. In most west African countries where plantation agriculture never took root, the recent investments in large-scale farming, e.g. in Ghana and Nigeria, have focused on food production.

While thus there is no correlation across Africa between export crops and large farms, there is evidence from most countries that better-off farmers tend to be more dependent on export crops than poorer farmers. It follows from this, and this is the third point, that the trends in producer prices have contributed to greater intrarural equality of income distribution. In several countries, especially in west Africa, there is a tendency towards regional specialization in food and cash crop cultivation. The richer coastal areas derive a larger proportion of their income from export crops than the poorer hinterlands, which rely more on cultivation of food crops. The relative position of the latter would therefore have been improved as a result of the price trends in the 1970s and early 1980s. Among the food producers it is the surplus farmers who would have derived the greatest benefit from an improvement in the real producer prices of food crops. In some countries a significant proportion of poor farmers may also be net food purchasers, whose incomes would suffer from rising food prices.

To go beyond these extremely broad generalizations, it is necessary to examine the producer price trends and their equity impact in individual countries. For this purpose, we utilize the fourfold classification of countries according to price trends in main food and export crops. The first category includes countries where real producer prices rose for the majority of the selected food and export crops. Kenya, Zambia, and Zaire fall in this category. The situation in Kenya and Zambia is analyzed in more detail later. Here it should be noted that this scenario represents the most favorable outcome for the rural sector as a whole. Farmers who are net surplus food producers and also export crop producers obviously benefit, providing their volume of output does not deteriorate sufficiently to offset the price rises. Farm workers and small farmers who are net food purchasers might be worse off on account of rising food prices, but improved prices are likely to generate an increase in the volume and remuneration for employment sufficiently to offset food price rises.

The distribution of benefits among farmers depends critically upon patterns of land ownership and spread of supporting public services. In Kenya, for example, the bulk of the benefits of improved production and prices has gone to large farmers and small growers in settlement schemes and in other high potential areas. Farmers in marginal and low-potential areas appear to have derived relatively few, if any, gains.[8] In Zambia, the bulk of benefits from increases in food production has accrued to large commercial farmers and those along the rail line.[9]

The second category with rising food crop but declining real cash crop prices includes Niger, Burkina Faso, Cameroon, the United Republic of Tanzania, Madagascar, Ghana, and possibly Nigeria. Surplus food producers will obviously benefit provided the volume of output is maintained or does not fall sufficiently to offset the price rise. These may be larger small farmers growing food crops for subsistence, or commercial small or large farmers specializing in food crops. In some countries these will be concentrated in certain regions or ecological zones. Small farmers growing a food surplus together with export crops may be better or worse off depending on the balance of the two sectors and the extent to which the decline in export crop prices can be offset by a volume increase. However, producers growing mainly export crops who cannot increase their marketed volume will be worse off, particularly if they are net food purchasers. One way of alleviating their position is for predominantly export crop producers to switch their resources to food crop production if this is possible. Workers for export crop producers, e.g. workers on plantations, will be worse off if they are paid in cash and wages are not increased. Moreover, employment opportunities may decline as well if the profitability declines as a result of the fall in real price.

Although there is a good deal of country and regional variation, on the whole it would seem that the larger farmers derive a higher proportion of their income from export crops than smaller, more subsistence-oriented farmers. Thus, one of the effects of the price shift in favor of food crops may be to promote greater equality among agricultural producers. Furthermore, in many west African countries there is a particularly marked division between production of food and export crops by ecological regions. In Ghana, for instance, cocoa is cultivated in the coastal belt while the northern savanna region specializes in food production. Thus the shift in prices in favor of food has resulted in a corresponding shift of income to the northern region.

The third category—rising export crop and declining food prices—includes Malawi, Sierra Leone, Zimbabwe, and Senegal. This situation will benefit specialist export crop producers such as plantations, together with predominantly export crop producers. All net food purchasers, farmers, and workers, will also benefit from this scenario. The group that appears to suffer most are surplus food producers, who may be the larger small farms or commercial food producers. In countries where food crops are produced in different areas to export crops there can also be distinct regional equity considerations in this situation.

Again the distribution of benefits depends a good deal on concentration in land ownership and production patterns. In Zimbabwe, for instance, during this period the bulk of commercial production, for both food and export crops, came from large, European farmers. In Malawi the plantations specialized in export crops while the bulk of surplus food sales came from "progressive" smallholders. Although the volume of employment on estates increased rapidly and this clearly spread the benefits to larger numbers of rural households, the real wages of estate workers declined in most years. Thus, while rising export prices benefited plantations and commercial farmers, the decline in food producer prices was not translated into lower consumer prices.

The final category includes countries with declines in real producer prices for both food and export crops. Somalia, Côte–d'Ivoire, and the Central African Republic fall in this category. This scenario is clearly the worst for the rural sector. Both surplus food producers and/or export crop producers are worse off, and agricultural employment is also likely to be adversely affected unless production increases to offset the price decreases. The income inequality in rural areas would depend on the relative incomes of predominantly food or cash crop growers and the relative decline in prices for these crops.

• EQUITY IMPACT OF AGRICULTURAL PRICE CHANGES: ILLUSTRATIONS FROM SOME COUNTRY EXPERIENCES •

This section examines in somewhat greater detail the equity impact of agricultural price trends in Kenya, the United Republic of Tanzania, Malawi, and Zambia. Within the limits of the data available, there is first a brief discussion of the structure of income distribution and of agricultural production. This information is then used to analyze the equity impact of agricultural price changes with focus on the main poverty groups.

Kenya

While it is difficult to estimate accurately the change in income distribution, it is generally agreed that there is considerable inequality in income distribution in Kenya. The gini coefficients for overall income distribution have been variously estimated in the mid-1970s between 0.5 and 0.60.[10] One estimate of household income distribution among urban households, smallholders, and other rural households gave gini coefficient figures of 0.52, 0.38, and 0.68, respectively.[11] While the extent of inequality among smallholders is moderate, the inclusion of the large farm and the plantation sector makes the overall rural income distribution quite unequal. One index of this is that the gini coefficient of land distribution in rural areas has been estimated at around 0.80, with the top 10 percent of the people accounting for 73 percent of the total land (this of course includes land held by companies and plantations also), and the bottom 60 percent for 7 percent. In the mid–1970s the proportion of the households suffering from poverty was estimated at 30-35 percent with rural poverty at around 35 percent and urban poverty at 25 percent. The main poverty groups are constituted by unskilled and semi-skilled workers in the formal and informal rural and urban areas, the landless (around 12 percent of rural households), the pastoralists (10 percent of total population), and smallholders with tiny holdings and in marginal areas.

Agricultural production is organized in a dualistic manner. The large farm sector consists of mixed farms, plantations, and ranches, owned by either individuals or companies. The smallholders, who comprise 80 percent of the total population in the country, cover a wide range of holdings varying in size from less than 0.5 hectare to 20 hectares. However, the majority of holdings have less than 2 hectares; for instance, in 1976–1977, nearly 75 percent of the holdings were estimated at below 2 hectares, with only 7 percent of 5 or more hectares. The share of the small farm sector in total marketed production rose rapidly in the 1960s but has fluctuated between 50 and 55 percent since the late 1960s.

As far as total marketed production is concerned, export crops are far more important than food crops. Excluding livestock and related products, in 1981–1982 cereals and sugar cane accounted for 16 percent of the total officially marketed output of crops. Furthermore, this ratio has fallen from 33 percent in 1969–1970. On the other hand, the value of major export crops—coffee, tea, sisal, pyrethrum—amounted to 84 percent of total marketed crop production in 1981–1982, having risen from 67 percent in 1969–1970. The breakdown of marketed production between smallholders and large farmers for individual crops is not available for recent years but was 45:55 in 1981. While some crops such as tea, coffee, maize, and sugar cane are grown by both sectors, cashew nuts and pyrethrum are grown almost exclusively by small farmers while sisal and wheat are grown exclusively or largely by large farmers. In 1981–1982 the smallholders were estimated to have produced 68 percent of the maize output, of which around 35 percent was marketed, this proportion varying from 1-16 percent for small farmers to 22-44 percent for intermediate holders and 67-85 percent for large holders. In 1983 smallholders accounted for 56, 32, and 44 percent of the coffee, tea, and sugar cane output, respectively.[12]

In light of the above information, what have been the main equity effects of agricultural price changes in the 1970s? Over 1968–1980 the relative consumer price of food tended to rise at a modest rate of 0.28 percent per year. Examination of retail prices of some major food items showed, as discussed in Chapter 7, that the relative price of sugar and maize rose while that of rice, wheat flour, and bread declined. The former have a heavier weight in the food expenditure of the rural and the poor as compared with urban and better-off groups. The rise in the relative consumer price of food thus had a proportionately stronger adverse effect on the low-income groups. In this connection, it is important to bear in mind that slightly less than 20 percent of those in gainful employment derive their livelihood primarily from wage employment, divided approximately in equal numbers between agriculture and other sectors. A significant proportion of such employees would be classified as working class. The other pertinent fact is that even in rural areas, rural agricultural workers and poor rural peasant households purchase nearly 46 percent of their food requirements and would, therefore, be affected by food prices.

Over the period 1968–1980, the rising wages for agricultural workers tended to cushion the adverse effects of an increase in relative food prices. Between 1968–1970 and 1978–1980, the real wages of agricultural workers went up by 33.3 percent. However, the real wages of non-agricultural employees over the same period declined by 5 percent. The impact on the urban poor was more severe since the real minimum wages fell by 12.6 percent. Between 1980 and 1983, the situation has worsened for most groups, the real agricultural, non-agricultural, and minimum wages having fallen by 39.5, 67.6, and 40 percent, respectively.

Coming now to the impact on the other major low-income group—the smallholders—the overall barter terms of trade for the agricultural sector have tended to decline in recent years, especially since 1978. However, there was a positive trend in the real producer prices for most food and export crops over the period 1968–1980. Relatively large increases accrued to producers of coffee, seed cotton, rice, and maize. But when the period is extended to 1983, the real producer prices for all crops except sugar cane show a negative trend, being relatively large for wheat, tea, pyrethrum, and rice. The pattern of price changes over either the period 1968–1980 or the period 1968–1983, does not show any relationship to producer categories. It does not, therefore, seem that the trends in real producer prices had any systematic bias in favor of or against small producers.

In summary, the rise in the relative price of food over 1968–1980 reinforced the decline in the real incomes of the urban poor but was not sufficient to offset the rise in money wages of agricultural workers. During the period the real producer prices rose for most products, with positive effects on farm incomes. However, the situation has deteriorated for all groups since 1980. When the period is extended to 1983, practically all producer prices showed negative trends.

There have been periods of food scarcity since 1970, but on the whole the transport and trade mechanisms have worked well enough to avoid extremes of shortages and rationing for long periods. Likewise, as far as one can tell, except for limited periods there has not been persistent disequilibrium between official producer and consumer prices and free market prices. Thus, the additional equity impact caused either by absolute scarcity and rationing of food or by divergent prices in the parallel markets appears to have been limited. This is of course not to deny that there have been periods such as in 1980 when food staples were in limited supply and actual consumer and/or producer prices much higher than the controlled prices. In such situations, as often happens, the urban population and especially the more affluent groups have better access to food and at more favorable prices.

Malawi

There are no reliable, recent figures on income distribution in Malawi. On the basis of the data available in 1967–1968, it was estimated that the bottom 40 percent of the population received 21 percent of total income while the top 10 percent received 40 percent.[13] The gini coefficient of urban income distribution in 1968 was estimated at 0.67, of estate workers at 0.28, and of the smallholder land distribution at 0.41.[14]

Malawi has experienced rapid economic growth since 1967–1968, and a number of important structural changes have taken place with significant impact on income distribution and living standards of low-income groups. Some of these changes include a sharp reduction in the number of migrant workers from Malawi to South Africa and rapid expansion in estate output and wage employment. It is not clear in what way the income distribution has been affected by the growth and changes of the past fifteen years. The important poverty groups consist of smallholders, accounting probably for 70-75 percent of the labor force; and unskilled employees and most informal sector operators in rural and urban areas. Perhaps 10 to 15 percent of the smallholders, described as "progressive" farmers, have achieved rapid increases in output and attained satisfactory income levels. The wage earners probably comprise about 15 percent of the labor force, the great majority being low-paid workers.

Agriculture is organized along dualistic lines. As of March 1979, the number of estates totaled 1,107. Of these 524 were flue-cured tobacco, 556 burley tobacco, 26 tea, and 1 sugar estate. These estates together contributed 15 percent of agricultural production and some 70 percent of agricultural exports in 1978. On the basis of the National Sample Survey of Agriculture, the number of smallholdings was estimated at 885,000 in 1964. Of these 28.7 percent were below 1.9 hectares and 63 percent below 4 hectares. Nearly 19 percent of the holdings had more than 6 hectares and 2 percent more than 12.

Consistent estimates of marketed output of agriculture are not available.[15] However, some idea of the importance of different crops and sectors may be obtained from ADMARC domestic purchases from smallholders and exports from estates. These purchases do not take into account private local sales and informal external trade in agricultural products. It should also be recalled that, as shown in Chapter 7, for most crops the price paid to growers is considerably below the sale price, and thus ADMARC purchase figures considerably underestimate the real contribution of smallholders to the total value of marketed production.[16] At the same time, we have figures on exports from estates but not total value of marketed production; the difference can be quite substantial for sugar, where nearly one third of the output is for domestic consumption. With these qualifications, it may be noted that nearly 50 percent of the export value from estates has come from tobacco in recent years (K.87.5 million in 1980), followed by sugar (K.36.3 million) and tea (K.30.3 million). The average purchase value by ADMARC of main crops has risen from kwacha 14.5 million in 1972–74 to kwacha 97.9 million in 1981–83.

Coming now to the equity impact of agricultural price changes, it may be recalled that the relative consumer price of food tended to increase by 0.8 percent per year over the period 1969–1980. Examination of basic food items in Chapter 7 showed that except for sugar and bread, the relative price of all other staple foods such as maize, rice, groundnuts, and cassava went up, the increase being particularly high for rice and maize. This had an adverse effect on the living standards of the wage earners, who in 1976 constituted about 17.2 percent of the labor force. The real wages in the agricultural and non-agricultural sectors fell by 22.0 percent and 22.2 percent between 1968–1970 and 1978–1980. The statutory minimum wage in real terms declined even more sharply, it fell by 41.7 percent between 1968–1970 and 1976–1978.

The trend in real producer prices over the period 1968–1980 was negative for tobacco, paddy, cassava, maize, and sugar cane while it was positive for groundnuts and tea. This picture remains essentially unchanged when extended to 1983, except that the size of the negative value for maize declined substantially. As noted in Chapter 7, the operations of the state marketing agency have had the effect of substantially taxing smallholder growers of export crops (tobacco, groundnuts, cotton) and of subsidizing producers and consumers of food crops (maize and rice). It has been estimated that in 1977–1978, the gross extraction per peasant worker was 23 kwachas, which represented one third of the average per head income of the poorest 90 percent of the population.[17] Using a different methodology, estimates made of the barter terms of trade faced by peasants show a decline from 104 in 1968–1970 to 97 in 1976–1978; the decline is sharper, from 102 to 88, if food prices are not excluded from the cost of living index.[18] The biggest impact of the adverse real producer prices must have been on the real incomes of "emergent" or "progressive" farmers since they derive a higher proportion of their cash income from sales of farm products.

To summarize the equity impact of agricultural price trends, the increase in the relative price of food has contributed to declining real wages for unskilled workers in urban and rural areas. Likewise the decline in real producer prices of most peasant crops, especially those exported, has adversely affected peasant incomes; the proportionate impact has been more on "progressive" farmers.

Zambia

Three features of the Zambian economy, noted in Chapter 7, are particularly relevant in discussing the equity impact of agricultural price changes. First, although agriculture accounts for a mere 12-14 percent of gross domestic product, close to 67 percent of the labor force derive their livelihood from agriculture. Secondly, a relatively high proportion of the population, estimated at between 40-45 percent in 1982, live in urban areas. Thirdly, wage employment constituted in 1978 nearly 22 percent of the total labor force.

Incomes are distributed quite unevenly. On the basis of the 1976 Household Budget Survey, it has been estimated that the poorest 40 percent of the population received 8 percent of total income while the richest 5 percent accounted for 35 percent of total income. The gini coefficient of income distribution was estimated at about 0.48 in both rural and urban areas, with an overall estimate at 0.59. Nearly 60 percent of the households were estimated to have incomes below "basic needs level": 80 percent in rural and 25 percent in urban areas.[19] As noted in Chapter 7, there has been a sharp decline in per head income since 1974, by nearly 50 percent. Thus, the living standards of all major socioeconomic groups have declined substantially over the past decade, although it is not known how income distribution has changed. The major poverty groups are predominantly subsistence farmers—about 75 percent of all farmers—and unskilled wages earners and employees in the informal sector.

The organization of production displays some dualistic features as shown in Chapter 7. While wheat is grown mostly by large commercial farmers, peasants provide the bulk of sorghum, groundnuts, and seed cotton. On the other hand, the sales of maize are shared more evenly between commercial farmers, large and small, and the peasants. A survey of 680 rural households all over Zambia carried out by Marter and Honeybone shows that cotton and sunflower, both cash crops, are grown largely by better-off peasants while the opposite is the case with sorghum and cassava. While millet is grown by an approximately similar proportion of households of different cash income groups, there is a tendency for a larger proportion of "richer" peasants to grow maize and groundnuts.[20] The same study also shows a higher concentration of brewing and fishing among the poorer farmers. The survey further brought out the differences between the central, southern, and eastern and the other provinces. In the more favored areas (central, southern, and eastern) the major crop for all groups was maize, with cash crops such as cotton and sunflowers becoming significant for the two richer groups. In the other areas cassava was the major crop, followed by maize and a range of minor crops such as groundnuts, millet, and sorghum.

Turning now to the impact on equity of changes in agricultural prices, it may be recalled from Chapter 6 that the relative consumer price of food increased by 0.57 percent per year over the period 1969–1980. In terms of individual food items, the relative price of rice fell sharply while that of maize rose substantially over the period 1974–1980. Rice is consumed primarily in urban areas while maize is the staple crop throughout the country and is consumed particularly by low-income groups. The real wages have fluctuated a good deal over the period 1968–1980, but the average for 1978–1980 does not diverge significantly from the average for the period 1968–1970 for agricultural and non-agricultural employees. However, since 1980 the real wages have fallen sharply.

Coming now to the impact on producers, the overall barter terms of trade for agriculture rose until 1972 but fell in the subsequent period to 1979. Between 1970 and 1979, the terms of trade fell by 20 percent.[21] In terms of individual crops, the trend in real prices over 1968–1980 was negative for sugar cane, paddy, and maize but positive (and large) for seed cotton and wheat. Extending the period to 1983 reduces the negative value for sugar cane and paddy and makes the price trend for maize a positive one. In terms of marketed output, maize is by far the most important crop. The share of maize in the total value of all crops marketed through official channels rose from 65 percent in 1970–1971 to 75 percent in 1980–1981. In 1982–1983, marketed output of maize was K.90.9, as compared with K.16.1, K.6.0, and K.5.8 (1980–1981) for sugar cane, seed cotton, and tobacco, respectively. Since maize is predominantly produced and marketed by smallholders, the producer price trends for maize over 1968–1980 had a significant adverse effect on their cash incomes. Other changes in the pattern of producer price changes have favored large and emergent commercial farmers. Cassava, sorghum, and groundnuts are more important to poorer peasants, and the producer prices of these products have fallen or risen less rapidly than those of crops grown predominantly by large and better-off smallholders.

To summarize the overall picture, the rise in real consumer food prices adversely affected low-income employees, who probably constituted one fifth of the labor force. The pattern of these price increases probably had a stronger adverse effect on the real incomes of the poorer sections of the population. It seems also likely that the pattern of real producer price changes affected poorer farmers more adversely. However, since 1980 the real producer prices for most agricultural crops have increased sharply, with beneficial effects on farmers' incomes.

United Republic of Tanzania

Although a number of attempts have been made to estimate the structure and trends in income distribution in the United Republic of Tanzania, these suffer from serious methodological and data deficiencies.[22] According to an ILO source, in 1976–1977 the top 10 percent of the households in rural areas accounted for 38 percent of cash income, the bottom one third for 9 percent. If subsistence production were included, the inequality would be considerably reduced. The comparable figures for urban income distribution were 34 and 11 percent, respectively. Furthermore, it was estimated that the income distribution became more even in both the sectors between 1969 and 1976–1977, the gini coefficient falling from 0.57 to 0.49 in rural areas (only cash incomes) and from 0.51 to 0.44 in urban areas. The rural-urban income gap declined in the 1970s: the ratio of average non-agricultural wages to average smallholder income was estimated at 2.5 in 1969, 2.9 in 1973–1975, and 1.4 in 1980.[23] It may be of interest to note that another source estimates the gini coefficient of land distribution among a sample of smallholders at 0.32.[24]

In terms of structure of agricultural production, smallholders are estimated to account for about 70 percent of total agricultural output. As far as marketed output is concerned, wheat, sisal, sugar, and tea are exclusively or predominantly estate crops, while 50 percent of rice comes from this sector. On the other hand, maize, tobacco, pyrethrum, cashews, coffee, cotton, drought staples, and legumes are marketed largely by small and medium farmers. As for the pattern of agricultural price changes, it will be recalled that the real consumer price of food rose at a relatively high rate of 1.71 percent per year over the period 1969–1980. Of the main staples, the relative prices of wheat and rice went up while that of maize meal declined quite sharply. If the period is extended to 1983, the real price of all cereals declined. Since maize is by far the most important staple, especially for low-income groups, it would appear that the adverse effect on the real incomes of the poor was probably less than indicated by the overall rise in food prices. On the other hand, as indicated in Chapter 7, in recent years there has been an increasing divergence between official and parallel market prices of most foodstuffs. The crucial question thus is the extent to which consumers make their purchases in parallel markets and the access to food at official prices of different categories of people.

Unfortunately, little evidence is available on either of these aspects. It has been estimated that 75 percent of the food requirements of Dar es Salaam inhabitants are met from the rationing system, but the ratio is lower in other towns. Nothing is known on the access of different income groups to food at official prices. It may be presumed that the rural population, to the extent that it purchases food to meet its requirements, may be able to do so on more advantageous terms. It may also be presumed that most higher income groups in urban areas would be able to secure access to food at official prices. It follows, therefore, that the urban poor are most likely to have to purchase food in the parallel markets.

Rising food prices have clearly contributed significantly to the declining real incomes of wage earners. The number of employees in recent years has amounted to about 7 percent of the labor force, the great majority of whom are employed in the non-agricultural sector. The real incomes of employees fell sharply in the 1970s. The real minimum wages fell by 24 percent between 1969–1970 and 1979–1980 and fell further by 40 percent between 1980 and 1983. Thus, in 1983 real minimum wages were 45 percent of the level in 1969. The average real non-agricultural wage fell even more rapidly, from Sh.381 in 1969 to Sh.198 in 1980, or by 48 percent. The 1983 real wage was a mere 35 percent of the 1969 level.[25]

What has been the impact on producer incomes of changes in relative agricultural prices? One aggregate measure of this is provided by the barter terms of trade. These show that the agricultural terms of trade declined practically every year except for 1976–1977. Between 1970 and 1980, the terms of trade declined by between 30 and 35 percent, depending on the cost of living index used.[26] The decline continued until 1983–1984. The fall in the index of export crops was even higher. For food crops there was an improvement from 1974–1975 for some years, but the decline after 1977–1978 offset most of the earlier gains. One observer has estimated that the changes in the barter terms of trade for peasant producers between 1970 and 1980 resulted in resource transfer out of the peasant economy amounting to nearly 27 percent of the sector output and that the proportion rose steadily over the period, to reach 38 percent in 1980.[27]

In terms of individual crops, the trend in real producer prices over 1968–1980 was negative for all export crops except coffee and was positive for most food crops except cassava. Extending the period to 1983, the positive values are reduced, the negative values increase, and several products, such as wheat, sorghum, and sugar cane change signs from positive to negative. In this connection, it is worth noting that export crops are far more important as sources of cash income than food crops, the average for 1981–1982 to 1983–1984 being Sh.1957 million versus Sh.436 million, or about four times as much. Thus, the impact on real incomes of farmers of adverse price trends for export crops has been proportionately much greater, although better coffee prices have moderated the decline in view of its importance as a cash crop. On the other hand, the better–off farmers are relatively more dependent on export crops,[28] and thus the pattern of price trends contributed to greater equality among producers. Comparing smallholders and estates, whether public or private, the pattern of price trends does not show any bias. This is because both smallholders and estates grow food as well as export crops; for instance, the bulk of the production of wheat, sugar, and rice comes from estates.

Finally, we consider the impact on equity of the operation of the parallel markets. It was noted earlier that the scope for transactions in parallel markets is more limited for export than for food crops. Thus the parallel market has served further to improve the relative producer food prices. In that sense it may have contributed to a more even rural income distribution. However, as between food producers, it is not possible to say whether there is a relationship between the proportion of sales to parallel markets and the cash income derived from food sales.

In summary, the sharp rise in real consumer food prices has contributed to a drastic reduction in the real incomes of urban and rural employees, although the decline in official retail maize prices shielded the poorest groups from the full impact of the rise in the overall food index. In recent years, the shortages of basic food items and the divergence in food price in parallel markets from the official levels may have especially depressed the living standards of the urban poor. The pattern of change in real producer prices has been particularly detrimental to export crop growers, though all farmers have suffered in varying degrees from deteriorating terms of trade.

• SUMMARY •

Because of the lack of data it has not been possible to undertake a comprehensive analysis of the equity impact of agricultural price changes. The analysis made here is partial and focuses only on the direct, first–round effect of price changes. Even within such a limited framework, the lack of adequate information on the structure of income distribution and patterns of production in most cases prevents the drawing of firm conclusions on the extent and sometimes the direction of the equity impact. The contribution of this chapter should be seen to lie in the approach and framework suggested for such analysis and in pointing to some broad consequences of changes in real agricultural prices. We hope that this effort will spur others to undertake a more in-depth and complete analysis of this vital but largely neglected aspect of food and agricultural policies.

A dominant feature of the price scene in the seventies has been the rise in real consumer food prices in most African countries. Of the eleven countries examined, the welfare impact has been most adverse in Ghana and Sierra Leone and most favorable in Mauritius, Swaziland, and Zimbabwe. The experience with real producer prices has been more diverse, with a pronounced tendency for the real price of food crops to rise and of export commodities to fall, especially if the analysis is extended to the early eighties. In most cases this pattern of price changes has contributed to greater equality in rural income distribution even when average rural incomes have fallen, as they have tended to in several countries, because of both poor production experience and declines in real prices of cash crops. The gap between the incomes of peasants and urban workers may also have been reduced in many countries as the workers' real incomes were depressed even more, in part because of rising food prices. There did not appear to be a general tendency for crop specialization by large and small farms, nor a tendency for price trends to be biased systematically in favor of large farms. There are, however, some cases where such tendencies were operative.

The more detailed analysis of the situation in four countries—Kenya, Malawi, Zambia, and the United Republic of Tanzania—confirmed some of these findings. The sharp declines in the incomes of urban workers were observed in all countries. Except in Malawi, there was no association between export crops and large farms. Nor did the price trends correlate in any systematic manner with farm size. The differential access to markets of consumers and producers of differing sizes and in different areas and the prevalence of different types of markets with different prices appear to be an increasing phenomenon in most countries with significant impact on income distribution and equity. Unfortunately, little is known of the quantitative dimensions of this aspect of markets and prices.

• NOTES •

1. This is to argue not that such situations and practices are non-existent in Africa but that their incidence and impact is severely limited in terms of areas and people affected.

2. Dharam Ghai, "Stagnation and Inequality in African Agriculture," in A. Maunder and K. Okhawa, eds., *Growth and Equity in Agricultural Development* (London: Gower, 1983); Dharam Ghai and Samir Radwan, eds., *Agrarian Policies and Rural Poverty in Africa* (Geneva: ILO, 1983); ILO/JASPA, *Rural-Urban Gap and Income Distribution: A Comparative Sub-Regional Study* (Addis Ababa: ILO/JASPA, 1983).

3. Polly Hill, *Studies in Rural Capitalism in Africa* (Cambridge: Cambridge University Press, 1970).

4. Paul Clough, "Farmers and Traders in Hausaland," *Development and Change* (London) 12, no. 2 (April 1981).

5. Paul Collier and Deepak Lal, *Poverty and Growth in Kenya*, Staff Working Paper No. 389 (Washington, D.C.: World Bank, 1980).

6. Amartya Sen, *Poverty and Famines* (Oxford: Clarendon Press, 1981); and G. Jan van Apeldoorn, *Perspectives on Drought and Famine in Nigeria* (London: Allen and Unwin, 1981).

7. For a discussion and application of one such methodology, see John W. Mellor, "Food Price Policy and Income Distribution in Low-Income Countries," *Economic Development and Cultural Change* (October 1978).

8. This is as true at the end of the decade as at the beginning. See, for instance, ILO, *Employment, Incomes and Equality: A Strategy for Increasing Productive Employment in Kenya* (Geneva: ILO, 1972); and I. Livingstone, *Rural Development, Employment and Incomes in Kenya* (Addis Ababa: ILO/JASPA, 1981).

9. C. Elliott, "Equity and Growth: An Unresolved Conflict in Zambian Rural Development," in Ghai and Radwan, *Agrarian Policies.*

10. See J. Vandemoortele and R. Van der Hoeven, *Income Distribution and Consumption Patterns in Urban and Rural Kenya*, Mimeographed World Employment Programme research working paper; restricted (Geneva: ILO, 1982); E. Crawford and E. Thorbecke, *Employment, Income Distribution, Poverty Alleviation and Basic Needs in Kenya* (Geneva: ILO, 1979); P. Collier and D. Lal, *Poverty and Growth in Kenya* (Washington, D.C.: IBRD, 1980); D. Ghai, M. Godfrey, F. Lisk, *Planning for Basic Needs in Kenya* (Geneva: ILO, 1978); and V. Jamal, *Rural Urban Gap and Income Distribution: The Case of Kenya* (Addis Ababa: JASPA, 1982).

11. Vandemoortele and Van der Hoeven, *Income Distribution.*

12. Republic of Kenya, *Economic Survey* (Nairobi: Central Bureau of Statistics, 1984).

13. World Bank, *World Development Report 1984* (Washington, D.C.: World Bank, 1984).

14. Dharam Ghai and Samir Radwan, "Agrarian Change, Differentiation and Rural Poverty in Africa: A General Survey," in Ghai and Radwan, *Agrarian Policies.*

15. Kydd and Christiansen, in "Structural Change in Malawi Since Independence," *World Development* (May 1982), have estimated the ratio of the *value* of estate

production to the value of the *officially marketed* peasant production as follows for selected years:

1969	1.21	1977	1.58
1971	1.12	1978	1.68
1973	1.44	1979	1.93
1975	1.76	1980	2.07

16. The implications for growth rate of marketed output may be different for different crops. Kydd and Christiansen have remarked in this context: "Since there is evidence that the share of official purchases in the total marketed surplus of staple crops has increased in the 1970s, the actual growth rates of total marketed surplus are lower than those shown . . . in the case of rice and maize. For other important peasant crops the growth rates are a tolerably accurate representation of actual production trends. . . ."

17. Ibid.

18. Ghai and Radwan, "Growth and Inequality: Rural Development in Malawi 1964–78," in D. Ghai and S. Radwan, *Agrarian Policies.*

19. JASPA, *Zambia: Basic Needs in an Economy Under Pressure* (Addis Ababa: ILO/JASPA, 1981).

20. A. Marter and D. Honeybone, *The Economic Resources of Rural Households and the Distribution of Agricultural Development* (Lusaka: Rural Development Studies Bureau, 1976).

21. JASPA, *Zambia: Basic Needs.*

22. A number of such attempts and their weaknesses are discussed in V. Jamal, *Rural Urban Gap and Income Distribution: The Case of Tanzania* (Addis Ababa: JASPA, 1982).

23. Ibid.

24. Paul Collier, Samir Radwan, and Samuel Wangwe, with Albert Wagner, *Ujamaa and Rural Development: Labour and Poverty in Rural Areas of Tanzania* (Oxford: Oxford University Press, 1985).

25. V. Jamal, *Rural Urban Gap, Tanzania;* and updated in an internal report on Tanzania by the same author, "Political Economy of Devaluation in Tanzania" (Geneva: ILO, 1984, mimeographed internal paper).

26. F. Ellis, Agricultural Marketing and Peasant State Transfers in Tanzania, *Journal of Peasant Studies* 10, no. 4 (July 1983).

27. Ibid.

28. Paul Collier et al., *Ujamaa and Rural Development.*

·9·

Principal Conclusions and Policy Implications

I n this chapter we summarize the principal findings of the study and spell out some implications for analysis and policy. We first take up the issue of the dimensions, nature, and underlying causes of the agricultural crisis in sub-Saharan Africa.

· MANIFESTATIONS AND DIMENSIONS OF CRISIS ·

There are various manifestations of the crisis, and different people have chosen to highlight its different aspects. At its most fundamental level, the crisis is reflected in the increasing numbers suffering from hunger and malnutrition. While precise figures on this cannot be expected, the number of severely hungry and malnourished people is estimated to have increased from 80 million in 1972–1974 to 100 million in 1984. At another level, the crisis is manifested in a deceleration of the rate of agricultural growth from 2.5 percent per year in the 1960s to 1.4 percent in the 1970s and early 1980s. More seriously, per head agricultural production declined by 1.1 percent per year in the 1970s.

The poor agricultural performance is in turn reflected in some other alarming indices such as an increase in the volume of food imports from 9 percent per year in the 1960s to 12.3 percent per year between 1969–1971 and 1980–1982 and to 19.9 percent per year in the more recent period of 1977–1979 to 1980–1982. At the same time, the volume of agricultural exports in 1977–1979 was at the same level as in 1961–1963 and fell by 3.5 percent per year over 1971–1980. In combination with an increase in population growth from 2.5 percent per year in the 1960s to 2.7 percent in the 1970s and high rates of growth of urbanization that rose from 5.3 percent in the 1960s to 5.9 percent per year in the 1970s, this poor agricultural performance has perforce resulted in rising consumer food prices in most countries.

It is clear that of the various manifestations of agricultural crisis, the low and declining rate of growth of agricultural output is the most significant. No appreciable progress can be made in the reduction of poverty, hunger, and malnutrition without a reversal in this trend. Nor can one expect much of an improvement in overall economic growth in most countries without a substantial increase in the rate of growth of agricultural output.

The preceding remarks on the dimensions of the agricultural crisis carry some implications for its nature. The evidence reviewed in the study suggests that the crisis is of a long–term nature, and it is clear that by the early 1970s the decline in growth rate was already under way. There is some, admittedly inadequate, evidence to suggest that the deceleration in growth may already have begun in the mid-1960s. If this interpretation is along broadly correct lines, it has important implications for both the diagnosis of the crisis and the solutions proposed to cope with it. One immediate implication of this interpretation is that while exogenous circumstances such as periodic drought or prolonged civil disturbances may trigger widespread famine and starvation, the underlying reasons for the food problems must be sought in more enduring factors.

Another aspect of the crisis that needs to be highlighted is its widespread geographical coverage. While one of the contributions of this study is paradoxically to demonstrate diversity in country situations and performances, the evidence presented here clearly points to the conclusion that a large number of countries have exhibited in varying degrees the manifestations mentioned earlier. The widespread occurrence of agricultural problems would suggest a pattern of causes with a wide sweep.

• THE UNDERLYING CAUSES •

These two aspects of the agricultural crisis—its long-term nature and its wide sweep—lead naturally to a discussion of its underlying causes. It must first be frankly admitted that despite widespread concern with the problem and the considerable efforts made by African governments, scholars, and the international community to come to grips with it, there continues to be a large measure of uncertainty and disagreement about the underlying factors, processes, and policies that have contributed to the crisis. Indeed, it might be said that while some agreement might be forthcoming on a list of the contributory causes, there are sharp divisions of view on both the relative importance of different factors and the precise mechanisms through which they have influenced the outcome. Given the deficiency of data on African economies, the enormous gaps in our knowledge of the agricultural systems, and the diversity of situations, it would be surprising if there were consensus.

Sometimes the differences among alternative explanations may be apparent rather than real and may derive from differences in language and modes of analysis. For instance, one school of thought argues that depressed domestic agricultural prices are at the heart of the agrarian difficulties in Africa. Another school of thought highlights the role of surplus extraction from the peasantry. The two explanations, while couched in different languages and deriving from totally different modes of analysis, may yet be in agreement on the central causes. Other examples of such apparent differences may be the explanations in terms of bloated civil services and deterioration in international terms of trade on the one hand, and exploitation by bureaucratic bourgeoisie and the operation of the world economic system on the other. The above remarks should not be interpreted to imply that the explanations offered by these contending schools of thought are identical. Indeed, their modes of analysis are profoundly different as are the underlying assumptions, theories of social change, and hence solutions offered. All that is claimed here is that there are common elements in their respective explanations that are often obscured by differences in language and modes of analysis.

This study does not purport to offer yet another explanation of the crisis. The objective has been to review alternative explanations and the evidence offered in their support. The hypotheses advanced range quite widely and incorporate several elements even though one or more factors may be highlighted as the major contributory causes. One type of explanation seeks the root of the crisis in the priority given to cash crops during the colonial era. While shedding some useful light on the current agricultural problems faced by a number of countries, it is clear that such an explanation cannot be wholly satisfactory, for not only did colonialism come to a formal end twenty to twenty-five years ago in most African countries but also the agricultural crisis comprises both cash and food crops. Indeed, the overall performance of the cash crop sector has been worse than that of the food sector.

A somewhat related explanation refers to neglect of agriculture during both the colonial era and the post-independence period. In one sense this must obviously be part of the explanation, but for it to have some operational value it is necessary to give some specific content to this hypothesis. The latter may be interpreted to mean two things: first, that the farmers have been faced with unfavorable and deteriorating terms of trade (the reference in popular discussions to low agricultural prices); and secondly, that the state expenditure, both capital and current, on agriculture and rural development has been low. The evidence presented in this volume on real price trends of agricultural commodities calls into question the simple and sweeping generalizations that are often made about agricultural prices. At the same time, the agricultural output is affected by so many factors that it is not surprising that most cross-country studies have failed to find a correlation between the growth of agricultural output and prices. This should not, however, be interpreted to imply that agricultural prices have no effect on output of individual crops.

One set of explanations revolves around the external economic relations of African countries. In specific terms, this explanation may be somewhat oversimplified to refer to trends in world commodity prices and to investment and the role of the multinational enterprises in agriculture. African countries have typically relied more heavily on export of agricultural commodities for generation of cash income, employment, and foreign exchange than other Third World regions, and in some countries foreign investment has been a significant factor in agriculture. The sharp deterioration in the terms of trade of most African countries in the late 1970s and early 1980s has without question aggravated the agricultural crisis, but its longer term nature as well as the different responses and performance of a large number of developing countries to this situation lead one to question the weight that might be given to the external factor. Nor does there appear to be any correlation between agricultural growth and foreign investment in the sector.

Some commentators have stressed the role of two exogenous factors in the agricultural crisis: the weather and political disturbances. Both these factors appear to have some validity for a group of countries. While there is no evidence of a secular deterioration of weather, it remains true that the Sahelian countries have suffered prolonged periods of drought in the 1970s and 1980s and a large number of eastern and southern African countries have been ravaged by failure of rains in successive years in the 1980s. But drought alone cannot explain the secular deterioration in growth of agricultural output or the wide reach and sweep of the crisis. Likewise, while it remains true that practically all the countries affected by prolonged internal or external conflicts and political instability have been among the worst performers in terms of agricultural growth, many countries that have escaped this fate have nevertheless not been able to surmount the crisis.

Finally, we consider the set of arguments associated with accelerating population growth and deterioration of environment. Undoubtedly, in a situation of fixity of land and static agricultural technology, rapid population growth can intensify agricultural problems through declining yields and productivity. But here again the evidence does not bear out the contention that countries with more rapid population growth have experienced lower growth in total or per head agricultural output.

The preceding discussion inevitably has done scant justice to the range, sophistication, and complexity of the hypotheses that have been advanced to explain the agricultural crisis confronting most African countries. Methodologically it is of course all too easy to knock down each hypothesis by advancing contrary examples. Furthermore, most statements advance a multiplicity of causes rather than single explanations. Nevertheless, it is useful to isolate the prominent hypotheses and to consider the evidence for their substantiation or rejection. One lesson that emerges from this study is that our understanding of the agricultural problems in Africa can be advanced only by detailed, in-depth analysis of the situation at the national and local levels. Only such an analysis can indicate the critical underlying factors behind deceleration in agricultural output and help us to separate the more important from the subsidiary causes.

• THE IMPORTANCE OF LABOR PRODUCTIVITY •

Whatever mode of analysis is adopted, it is clear that at a most general level the level and growth of agricultural output is likely to be determined largely by incentives and resources made available to the sector. The term "incentives and resources" covers a wide range of things such as attractive prices, access to inputs and consumer goods, efficient marketing and transport network, and adequate investment in research in technology in the broadest sense. The last point is particularly important in the context both of a rapidly changing agricultural system from shifting to settled agriculture and of the need to raise yields and productivity to ensure an attractive income to farmers. By all accounts the absence of suitable innovations in technological packages has been an important element in the failure to arrest the deceleration in agricultural growth.

A useful way to focus on agricultural problems and potentials in most African countries is through analysis of labor productivity. This study has shown that while a majority of countries has experienced some increases in agricultural labor productivity in the 1970s, the growth in most cases has not been sufficient to prevent a fall in per head agricultural output, taking into account the growth in overall population and agricultural labor force. Labor productivity is determined by a variety of factors including weather, irrigation, soil fertility, quality of labor force, management skills, use of inputs (such as fertilizers, pesticides, and herbicides), access to improved seeds, and quality of tools and equipment. Over the past decade or so the productivity-enhancing impact of these factors has not been sufficiently great to impart a strong dynamic impulse to agricultural growth. In fact, with respect to several of the crucial factors such as weather, soil fertility, and quality of labor force (owing to migration of the young and educated), the negative effects have predominated. At the same time the biological, chemical and mechanical innovations have either been lacking or have been too feeble sufficiently to offset the productivity–depressing factors and result in sustained enhancement of productivity. It is suggested that expenditure and policies on agriculture be reassessed with a view to effecting significant and sustained improvements in labor productivity. In this respect, the critical factors in the long run would appear to be biological and chemical innovations, improvements in implements and mechanical power, and spread of irrigation.

• THE DIVERSITY OF AGRICULTURAL SYSTEMS AND PERFORMANCE •

Although there is a tendency to talk in terms of *the* agricultural crisis in Africa, a tendency that seems justified by the large number of African countries facing agricultural problems, a remarkable fact about the African economies and agriculture is their diversity. This diversity is manifested at many levels, in natural and agricultural resources and in economic structure and performance.

The climatic differences are considerable and range both within and among countries from dry, desert-like situations found in the northern areas of the Sahelian countries to lush, wet, tropical forest zones characteristic of the coastal belt of the west African states; and from the low dry savannas of southern and eastern Africa to the cool, rainy highlands of eastern and central Africa. There is a corresponding diversity in the food systems, which comprise at least five main groups: millet and sorghum areas of the Sudano-Sahel group, rice in Madagascar and certain west African countries, the root crop areas in the central African region, areas mainly in west Africa where root crops and grains are of equal importance, and the maize-growing region of eastern and southern Africa.

There is also a surprising range in population density, varying from two persons per square meter in Botswana to 204 in Rwanda, the majority falling in the five to twenty-five bracket. More relevant from the agricultural point of view is the availability of arable land, which ranges from 12.5 hectares per head in the Congo to 0.2 in Rwanda. Although African countries may still be characterized in broad terms as land–abundant, it is instructive to note that in 1981 no fewer than twelve countries possessed less than 1 hectare of arable land per head of the population, while only six countries had more than 5 hectares. These figures are likely to continue to decline sharply with high rates of population growth. The cropping intensities also show sharp disparities, ranging in 1975 from less than 40 percent in fifteen countries to more than 70 percent in eight countries.

There are also pronounced differences in the size and rate of population growth. In 1981 Nigeria alone accounted for over 24 percent of the population of sub-Saharan countries. It is also interesting to note that six countries—Nigeria, Ethiopia, Zaire, Sudan, the United Republic of Tanzania, Kenya—had 57 percent of the total population. At the other end, fifteen countries with less than 5 million population accounted for less than 10 percent of the entire sub-Saharan population. A major implication of these disparities in population size is that performance in half a dozen or so large countries is critical for the continental average. The rates of population growth over the period 1967–1981 showed lesser variation, with most countries falling in the 2 to 3 percent per year rate, with fourteen countries with growth rates equal to or in excess of 3 percent and four countries with 2 percent or less.

More interesting from the point of view of this study are differences in economic structure and performance. In practically all countries, agriculture remains an extremely important source of livelihood for the labor force, with sixteen countries with a ratio of 80 percent or more and only two countries with less than 50 percent. The share of agriculture in gross domestic product shows greater variation, with figures in excess of 50 percent in six countries and less than 25 percent in ten countries. With respect to agricultural performance the two extremes are represented by six countries with growth rates in excess of 3 percent per year over the period 1969–1971 to 1979–1981 and by fifteen countries with rates of 0.6 percent and less. More revealingly, out of thirty-nine countries only six achieved a positive growth in per head agricultural output over this period and seven in per head food output. This is a measure of the wide geographical range of the agricultural crisis in Africa. We have not discussed economic and agricultural policies in their entirety, but the discussion in Part 2 showed that, at least with respect to pricing and marketing policies, there has been considerable variation in country experiences.

The preceding discussion on diversity not only corrects the widespread impression of similarity of agricultural conditions in sub-Saharan Africa, but more importantly points to the need to devise programs and policies geared to the specificity of each country and region.

• TRENDS IN REAL AGRICULTURAL PRICES •

One of the principal objectives of the study has been to document and analyze the trends in real agricultural prices in African countries in the 1970s. It is hoped that the data assembled here might provide the empirical foundation for more in-depth studies of the impact of agricultural prices on production and income distribution. We have attempted to calculate the trend in real producer and, where relevant, consumer prices for the major export and food crops over the period 1969–1980 for a large number of African countries. On several occasions we have pointed out the limitations and possible imperfections of the data, including the divergence between the official and actual producer and consumer prices, the existence of several markets with several prices, inadequacy of the cost-of-living index to deflate the nominal prices, etc. Despite these limitations, the data on price series in Africa are probably more reliable than most other series on agriculture and give a reasonable approximation of the broad patterns and trends in real agricultural prices. In this respect it should be noted that most of the price estimates presented here are *trend* averages. This has the advantage over other types of estimates more commonly quoted of ironing out year–to–year fluctuations over the period of a decade and of thus giving a picture of the *tendency* of price movements.

Three major conclusions may be drawn from estimates of price trends, all in varying degrees running counter to the conventional wisdom on the subject. The first conclusion is that in the 1970s real consumer food prices tended to rise in most African countries, a tendency observable in fourteen out of seventeen countries for which it was possible to estimate this statistic. The cost-of-living index used to make these estimates comprises both imported and local foods, but the latter have a predominant weight. In countries where the breakdown between local and imported foods is available, such as Ghana and Nigeria, the rise in prices of imported foods is much less than in those of local foods. This finding does not of course imply that consumer food prices are in any sense at optimum or equilibrium prices; one would need a separate exercise to provide an answer to this question. Nor does it contradict the frequently advanced statement that the consumer food prices are kept at a low level. But at the least it challenges the statement about continuances of cheap food policy. The data show that consumer food prices on the average tended to rise faster, and in some countries considerably faster, than the prices of other consumer goods and services.

We do not argue that the increase in the relative price of food is necessarily the result of a conscious policy decision to raise producer prices, either to give incentives to food production or to reduce or eliminate the expenditure on food subsidies. We see the increase in relative food prices rather as a market response, in some instances despite government policy, to persistent food shortages in relation to demand for food. As such it is more a reflection of failure of efforts to raise domestic food production than a policy response.

The second major finding in this area is that with respect to real producer prices there was a predominance of positive trends for food crops in most African countries and of negative trends for cash crops. This finding thus runs counter to the frequent generalization that cash crops have tended to receive preferential price treatment. Once again, however, one should not necessarily see in these trends a reflection of deliberate policy decisions. As shown later, real producer prices are determined by a variety of external and internal factors, some of which at least, such as world prices for exports or domestic production of foodstuffs, are beyond the direct control of governments. In this connection the study shows that for the five food crops examined, except sugar, there was a tendency for the ratio of domestic to world prices to rise in most countries. For the three export crops, the picture was more mixed. The overall result appears to indicate an effort to move closer to the world prices.

The third significant finding relates to the diversity of country experiences with respect to trends in producer prices. The attempt to classify countries into four groups in terms of the behavior of real producer prices for selected export and food crops yields some surprising results. The inclusion of a larger set of commodities with appropriate weighting may modify some of these results. Our results show Kenya and Zaire in the category of countries with positive price trends for both selected food and cash crops, with Somalia, Côte–d'Ivoire, and the Central African Republic in the opposite category of declining price trends. The largest category, comprising among others Niger, Burkina Faso, Cameroon, Ghana, the United Republic of Tanzania, and possibly Nigeria, includes countries with rising real producer prices for food crops and declining for export crops. The opposite tendency is seen in Malawi, Zimbabwe, Sierra Leone, and Senegal. Apparently such a pattern of price trends does not correlate with performance. At the least, therefore, the results show that real prices by themselves do not explain all. These results also contradict the stereotype that all African countries follow identical policies, resulting in a depression of real agricultural prices.

It would have been useful to go beyond estimation of price trends and delve into the objectives and mechanisms of agricultural price formation. Constraints of time and space have prevented such an analysis for a large number of African countries, but we have attempted to examine in more detail the experience in six countries—two each in east, central and west Africa—for the light they throw on pricing and marketing policies as well as on the recent changes in these areas.

• MARKETING AND PRICING POLICIES •

The six countries examined show considerable diversity with respect to the objectives of pricing policy, the marketing structures, and the mechanisms used to influence price levels and trends. Furthermore, in most countries there have been significant changes over time in marketing structures and price policies and instruments. A common pattern observed in all countries is the extensive and increasing involvement of the state in agricultural marketing and pricing through the 1970s. It is only since 1982 or so that there has been some reversal in this trend. However, the objectives and scope of state intervention have tended to vary by country and often over time.

In Kenya and Zambia the marketing boards were first created to provide protection for European agriculture and covered the staple foods. While in Kenya the protectionist tendency continued to dominate policy, in Zambia the predominance of mining interests soon shifted the concern of the government towards keeping low the price of basic foodstuffs. In Nigeria and Ghana, on the other hand, the marketing boards were created to siphon off surplus from the sale of export crops. In Malawi, the marketing board has effectively served as an instrument to extract surplus from the peasant production of export crops and to subsidize food crops. Finally, in the United Republic of Tanzania, state intervention and controls came as an essential part of a policy of an increasingly centrally planned economy and served also to extract surplus from peasant production. In eastern and central African countries the government policy did not make any distinction between food and export crops. The state role in pricing and marketing extended to all crops and, except for Malawi, did not distinguish between large and small farmers. In Ghana and Nigeria, despite recent attempts by the governments to extend state control over food crops, the policy has focused largely on export commodities.

All countries experienced a rise in the relative consumer price of food, but there was a great deal of variation with respect to real producer prices. In Kenya, the producer prices for the majority of both export and food crops tended to move up while, interestingly enough and contrary to what is generally believed, they tended to decline in Malawi. In Ghana and the United Republic of Tanzania, the real producer prices of the majority of food and export crops show opposite trends, the former rising and the latter falling. In Nigeria also this is the most probable scenario. It is difficult to classify Zambia along these lines as there are no major export crops. The real producer prices tended to decline for most of the important crops such as maize, tobacco, sugar cane, and paddy but rose for a few crops such as wheat and seed cotton.

The countries also display considerable diversity with respect to the mechanisms used to influence producer and consumer prices. While they all used direct price fixing with different degrees of success to determine agricultural prices, the influence of other mechanisms tended to vary. Increasing overvaluation of the currency was a factor in all countries, but its incidence was greatest in Ghana and Nigeria and lowest in Zambia and Malawi. Commodity taxes were important in Nigeria and Ghana but were phased out in the 1970s in the former. In the United Republic of Tanzania they also became important in the late 1960s and the 1970s. Kenya, Zambia, and Malawi did not use commodity taxes to any significant extent.

Nigeria and Ghana used surpluses by the marketing boards to extract additional resources from the agricultural sector. Malawi also resorted to this device to tax peasant agriculture. On the other hand, Kenya, Zambia, and the United Republic of Tanzania did not make use of this device to squeeze agriculture. Finally, the increasing inefficiencies and mismanagement of marketing boards appear to have been a common factor in all countries, albeit in varying degrees, in depressing producer prices.

The global recession and the growing agricultural crisis in Africa have led to significant changes in marketing and pricing policies in the 1980s. The governments have been attempting to provide more attractive producer prices and policies for agricultural crops, but in some cases these efforts have been frustrated by falling export prices and galloping domestic inflations. The governments in all countries have tended to place greater reliance on exchange rate flexibility as a policy instrument. Export taxes have been phased out in the United Republic of Tanzania and Ghana. In several countries—the United Republic of Tanzania, Ghana, Nigeria, and Zambia—the marketing boards have been incurring losses in recent years and receiving government subsidies. Finally, in most countries significant changes are being introduced in the marketing system designed to enhance efficiency by increasing the role of private traders and cooperatives and to reduce the monopoly exercised by state marketing boards.

• AGRICULTURAL PRICES AND EQUITY •

Changes in agricultural prices have wide-ranging equity effects, but this topic has been largely ignored in the literature on the subject, at least in part due to the lack of relevant information. A complete analysis of the equity impact of changes in agricultural prices requires data on patterns of income and asset distribution, sources of income, the structure of agricultural output by income or land size, and the patterns of expenditure. The analysis should also take into account both the direct and indirect effects of price changes through adjustments in consumption and production. Needless to say, it has not been possible to undertake such a comprehensive analysis. This study has for the most part focused on direct equity effects of price changes. Such generalizations as can be made on the continental experience are supplemented by more detailed analysis of the situation in four countries.

We first examined the equity impact of an increase in real consumer food prices in eleven African countries. Other things being equal, the adverse effects on welfare tend to be more serious with higher increases in relative food prices, lower income per head, greater concentration of income, larger size of the working class (i.e., those dependent on purchases to meet their food needs), and lower increases in money wages of low income workers. The rising food prices have had a particularly adverse impact on the real incomes of urban unskilled and informal sector workers. In many countries their incomes have fallen more sharply than those of farmers, and the rural income gap between workers and peasants has been greatly reduced. Of the countries examined, the overall welfare impact of changes in consumer food prices in the 1970s was the most adverse in

Ghana and Sierra Leone, followed by Côte–d'Ivoire, Malawi, the United Republic of Tanzania, and Zambia, and the most favorable in Mauritius, Swaziland, and Zimbabwe, followed by Kenya and Nigeria.

Changes in real producer prices have a direct impact on the incomes of farmers. As already noted, the experience with real producer prices has been more diverse with, however, a pronounced tendency for the real price of food crops to rise and of export commodities to fall, especially if the analysis is extended to the early 1980s. In most cases this pattern of price changes has contributed to greater equality in rural income distribution even when average rural incomes have fallen, as they have tended to in several countries because of both poor production experience and declines in real prices of cash crops. The gap between the incomes of peasants and urban workers may also have been reduced in many countries as the workers' real incomes were depressed even more, in part because of rising food prices. There did not appear to be a general tendency for crop specialization by large and small farms, nor a tendency for price trends to be biased systematically in favor of large farms. There are, however, some cases where such tendencies were operative.

The more detailed analysis of the situation in four countries—Kenya, Malawi, Zambia, and the United Republic of Tanzania—confirmed some of these findings. The sharp declines in the incomes of urban workers were observed in all countries. Except in Malawi, there was no association between export crops and large farms, nor did the price trends correlate in any systematic manner with farm size. The varying access to markets of consumers and producers of different sizes and in different areas, and the prevalence of different types of markets with different prices, appear to be an increasing phenomenon in most countries, with significant impact on income distribution and equity. Unfortunately, little is known of the quantitative dimensions of this aspect of markets and prices.

• SOME IMPLICATIONS FOR POLICY AND ANALYSIS •

At various points in the study we have drawn attention to the implications of our analysis for policy and research. Here we recapitulate some important points. The first one to emphasize is the complexity of the agricultural systems and our imperfect understanding of both the nature and dynamics of change and particularly the forces contributing to deceleration of agricultural growth. Policy measures must seek to halt and reverse the recent trends in agricultural production.

The policy response needs to be along two lines. The first relates to the urgent need to bring about significant and sustained increases in labor productivity. This in turn calls for an intensive effort to identify, develop, and implement appropriate biological, chemical, and mechanical innovations. In practically all cases this will necessitate increasing agricultural research at local, national, and regional levels. The second element in the policy response concerns incentives and resources for agricultural development, including coordinated improvements in the marketing and pricing environment. It has been argued in Chapter 5 that the pricing mechanism does not operate effectively in many situations because of inadequacies and bottlenecks in the markets for resources and goods. Removal of these may require substantial investment in rural transport infrastructure in some instances. In other cases, changes in licensing arrangements and administrative procedures may provide a sufficient incentive for local or private initiative and investment. We do not intend to provide an exhaustive catalogue of possible market improvements, but the identification of marketing constraints and the development of feasible methods for their removal is a fruitful area for both research and policy analysis.

It was also argued in Chapter 5 that the effectiveness of the pricing mechanism was weakened, and sometimes completely frustrated, by the lack of coordination between the authorities responsible for the various pricing instruments. Furthermore, all too frequently agricultural pricing decisions are taken in a partial equilibrium framework, whereas given the importance of the agricultural sector in many countries it is of considerable importance to consider the interaction of different pricing decisions and the macroeconomic implications of the various prices that impinge on the agricultural sector. These include the exchange rate, the rate of interest, and domestic agricultural sector barter terms of trade. This is a relatively neglected area of research in many sub-Saharan African countries, a situation not helped by the current dearth of skilled manpower devoted to price analysis and the lack of attention paid to price coordination.

We have also emphasized the need both for a fuller and deeper understanding of the critical factors behind the crisis and for in-depth research at the local and national levels. The dearth of reliable and adequate data on production, assets, and income distribution has been repeatedly stressed. Much of the post-war literature on development has focused on distribution and welfare in the context of growth. The African experience in the 1970s and the early 1980s indicates that an equally important topic is the distribution of income, consumption, and wealth in the context of stagnation and decline. There is also a pressing need for reform in the external economic environment—in price stabilization, aid programs, investment priorities, and access to markets in industrialized countries—but these have been explored in other fora. The present study has concentrated more on domestic policy issues and the action the African countries can take in a self-reliant spirit to break out of the current crisis.

Index

ADMARC. *See* Agricultural Development and Marketing Corporation
Agricultural crisis, 1–2, 7, 8, 155–156; causes, 39–40, 52, 156–159; colonial system and, 40–42; mismanagement, 49, 128
Agricultural Development and Marketing Corporation (ADMARC) (Malawi), 106, 107, 108, 109, 146
Agricultural extension services, 46
Agricultural policy, 2–3, 58. *See also* Public policy
Agricultural production, 12, 16, 23, 51, 57, 114, 124, 133, 155, 159; climate zones and, 31–34, 37; colonial system, 40–42; decline, 39, 156; diversity,160–161; growth rate, 24, 26–27; indicators, 12–14; Kenya, 143–144; Malawi, 105–106, 146; prices and, 52, 58, 61, 64, 135–136, 139–140, 157–158; Tanzania, 118–119, 149–150; Zambia, 109, 148; *See also* Agriculture; Cash crops; Consumer food prices; Food production; Prices; *individual crops*
Agricultural Rural Marketing Board (ARMB) (Zambia), 110
Agriculture, 8, 12, 47, 161; employment, 14, 23; technology, 44–46; urban migration, 14–15; *See also* Agricultural production; Cash crops; Food production; *individual crops*
Angola, 23, 30, 33, 34, 48, 134
ARMB. *See* Agricultural Rural Marketing Board

Beans, 114
Benin, 23, 32, 34
Botswana, 23, 33, 34, 132, 160

Burkina Faso, 32, 33, 78, 85, 134, 141, 163
Burundi, 23, 34, 133

Cameroon, 28, 134; agricultural production, 34, 76, 80; climatic zone, 32, 33; crop prices, 80, 95, 97, 99, 141,163
Capital intensive projects, 50
Cash crops, 40, 137, 141, 148, 157, 163; purchasing power, 98–100; real producer prices, 81–85; Tanzania, 118, 119; world prices, 81–85; *See also* Exports; Producer prices; *individual crops*
Cashew nut production, 118, 119, 122, 144, 150
Cassava production, 32, 114, 124; Malawi, 106, 107, 108, 146, 147; Tanzania, 118, 120, 151; Zambia, 109, 148
Central Africa, 32–33
Central African Republic, 28, 32, 34, 76, 81, 84, 85, 142, 163
Cereals production, 16–18, 28–30, 45, 117, 143. *See also* Maize production; Rice production; Wheat production
Chad, 23, 31, 32, 33, 48
Climate, 31–33, 37
Clove production, 118
Cocoa Marketing Board (Ghana), 124
Cocoa Marketing Board (Nigeria), 117
Cocoa production, 99, 114, 117, 124, 125, 132; prices, 81, 82–83(table), 84, 99
Coffee production, 32; Ghana, 124, 125; Kenya; 102, 105, 144, 145; prices, 81, 82–83(table), 84, 98–99; Tanzania, 118, 119, 122, 150, 151
Colonial systems; agricultural

production, 40–42, 133; infrastructure, 42–43; world economy, 43–44
Commodities, 63, 88–89, 91–92, 164. *See also* Exports
Communications systems, 42
Congo, the, 23, 30, 32, 34, 160
Consistent price index, 103
Consumer food prices, 3, 68–69, 106–108, 165; changes, 136–139, 151, 164; and producer prices, 69, 87–88, 103–104, 110, 111–112, 115–116, 120–122, 125, 127; *See also* Cost of living; Food prices; Income; Prices
Consumer price index, 19, 87, 103–104
Cost of living, 69, 87–88, 106–107, 162. *See also* Consumer food prices; Income
Côte–d'Ivoire, 28, 29, 32, 34, 140; cotton production, 84, 85; crop prices, 69, 98, 99, 139, 142, 163, 166; imports, 77, 78; income distribution, 132, 139
Cotton production, 99, 125, 145; Malawi, 107, 108; Nigeria, 114, 117; prices, 81, 82–83(table), 84–85; Tanzania, 118, 119, 123, 150; Zambia, 109, 110, 111, 113, 148, 149
Crop yields, 44–45. *See also* Agricultural production; Food production; *individual crops*

Dairy products, 18
Desertification, 15
Djibouti, 33
Droughts, 16, 48

East Africa, 33
Economic Committee (Tanzania), 119
Economic growth, 7–9, 11, 23–24, 49, 50
Economic system; mismanagement, 49–51; *See also* Marketing systems; Pricing systems; World economic system
Education, 42, 133
Effective rates of protection (ERP), 113
Employment. *See* Labor force
Environment, 47–48

Equity impact, 131, 152; agricultural prices, 134–136, 148, 149, 165–166; consumer food prices, 136–139; real producer prices, 139–143
ERP. *See* Effective rates of protection
Ethiopia, 33, 34, 35, 48, 80, 95, 97, 98, 134, 160
Exchange rates, 91–93, 165. *See also* Foreign exchange earnings
Exports, 44, 58, 78, 84, 123, 133, 140, 142, 158; agricultural, 13, 14, 26, 37, 41; Ghana, 124, 126; Kenya, 103, 143–144; Malawi, 107, 108–109; marketing, 126, 127; Nigeria, 114–115, 116, 117, 118; prices, 59, 63, 116, 117, 120, 162–163; Tanzania, 118, 120, 122, 123, 151; taxation, 122, 128, 165; *See also* Taxation; *individual crops*

Famines, 11
FAO. *See* Food and Agriculture Organization
Farming systems, 47–48. *See also* Agricultural production
FDC. *See* Food Distribution Corporation
Food and Agriculture Organization (FAO), 10, 12, 30, 33–34, 86
Food Distribution Corporation (FDC), 125
Food price index, 19, 115
Food prices, 12, 19, 146, 155; changes, 135, 141, 142, 144–145, 151; *See also* Consumer food prices; Prices
Food production, 13, 15, 16, 37–38, 45, 47, 118, 142; colonial period, 40–41; Ghana, 125, 126; growth rate, 20(n7), 24, 26–27; patterns, 33–34; prices, 59, 63–64, 68–69, 70–75(tables), 76, 105, 117; *See also* Consumer food prices; Food prices; Food supplies; *individual crops*
Food supplies, 47, 60, 66; availability, 30–31, 135, 150; consumption patterns, 33–34. *See also* Food production
Foreign exchange earnings, 59, 61, 80–81, 118. *See also* Exchange rates

About the Authors

Dharam Ghai is chief of the Rural Employment Policies Branch, International Labour Office (ILO). He has held teaching and research appointments at Makerere University, Yale University's Economic Growth Centre, and the University of Nairobi, and in 1970–1974 was director of the University of Nairobi's Institute for Development Studies (IDS).

Lawrence D. Smith is reader in agricultural economics in the Department of Political Economy and chairman of the Centre for Development Studies at the University of Glasgow. A senior research fellow at IDS in 1968–1971, he was a member of the ILO Employment Mission to Kenya in 1972 and is a frequent consultant for FAO on agricultural marketing and policy in Sub-Saharan Africa.